"Stay with us..."

Encounters *with the* Risen Lord

Reflections by **Fr. Thomas Rosica, CSB**

Foreword by **His Beatitude Michel Sabbah**
Latin Patriarch-emeritus of Jerusalem

TWENTY-THIRD PUBLICATIONS
twentythirdpublications.com

Cover image: The Emmaus icon on the cover and used throughout
the book was commissioned in 1990 by Fr. Thomas Rosica, CSB, and
written by Sr. Marie-Paul Farran, OSB, of the cloistered Benedictine
Monastery on the Mount of Olives in Jerusalem. The original icon is in
Toronto. Reproductions of the icon are available through the Printery
House in Conception, Missouri. Photo of original icon by Salt and
Light Catholic Media Foundation.

TWENTY-THIRD PUBLICATIONS
One Montauk Avenue, Suite 200
New London, CT 06320
(860) 437-3012 or (800) 321-0411
www.twentythirdpublications.com

ISBN: 978-1-62785-331-6
Library of Congress Control Number: 2017962961
Printed in Canada.

A division of Bayard, Inc.

Dedication

To the memories of

Cardinals Joseph Bernardin (1928–1996)
and Basil Hume, OSB (1923–1999)

Witnesses of the Risen Lord
who knew and loved the One in whom they hoped.

Through their living and dying,
they taught us more about Resurrection
than we could ever learn from books.

> *"My God, I know this place. I am home. Somehow I think crossing from this life into life eternal will be similar. I will be home."*

> —Joseph Bernardin, 1996

> *"The curtain came down and it was back to the darkness of faith. But I wasn't worried because I knew what was behind that curtain."*

> —Basil Hume, OSB, 1999

Contents

Foreword

F r. Thomas Rosica, a member of the Congregation of Priests of St. Basil (Basilian Fathers), is a Scripture scholar and the founding chief executive officer of the Salt and Light Catholic Media Foundation and Television Network. Though he has many other titles and responsibilities in the Canadian Church and in society, I believe that the best title for him is "lover of Jerusalem." I first met him in 1990, during his graduate studies at the École Biblique et Archéologique Française de Jérusalem, where I asked him to assist me in a special ministry with seminarians and parish priests, who always admired his teaching ability. But Fr. Rosica's main activity was his zeal to discover Jesus in his land. He discovered the Lord in the Holy Places which continue to preserve the memory of the mystery of God in the midst of men and women of all times.

This little book, entitled "*Stay with Us…*," is a collection of reflections on the Gospels and is the result of Fr. Rosica's years of prayer and studies in Jerusalem and in the Holy

Land – the land of the Gospel. The author lived here for some time to get to know Jesus Christ and his Gospel better. The biblical reflections in this book are the result of his prayer and his studies in the Land of Jesus. As he himself says in his introduction, "Many of those reflections matured while I lived and studied in Jerusalem." Throughout these reflections, the reader feels that Fr. Rosica has a certain nostalgia for the land and for his Lord, who made this land holy – the land of humanity's redemption.

He presents Jesus Christ, man and God, the eternal Word of God, to our modern world through the mystery of the cross. He says with St. Paul: "We preach Jesus Christ," the scandal and folly of the cross, in order to become mature men and women who can transcend the borders of humanity, and know, as the author says, that death or evil do not have the last word. The tragic, violent events of Good Friday are not the end of the story. Death is not the final answer. And God knows how many acts of violence and tragedies are woven into our daily lives even to this day. In the face of the mystery of evil, how many people simply lower their arms in despair and sentence themselves to not believing or seeing the mystery of God among us and within us!

Fr. Rosica has focused his reflections on the Lord who sanctified the land and has kept in the secret of his prayer the men and women who continue to suffer in that land, awaiting the redemption of Jerusalem and all its inhabitants who are still at war. Today it is still called the

Holy Land, even though it continues to be torn apart by a never-ending war among its two peoples. Someone who believes in the mystery of this land may sense a deadly connection between the holiness of the land and the evil of war that has continued through the centuries and is still lived here today by its inhabitants. Though it is the city of the redemption of the world, Jerusalem itself has not yet welcomed its redemption.

The author tells us that the Resurrection of Jesus Christ is the answer. The Lord has overcome death and evil. This is true. But what many men and women of our time are seeking is the resurrection in themselves, in their own lives, and in the history of so many countries at war, beginning with the Holy Land. A question and a drama which the author invites us to accept is the folly of the cross, so that we can conquer evil in and around us. Through their contribution, believers in our time bring a little more light and a little more love into the world.

Fr. Rosica proposes another reflection which can guide a human life. Every human being and every believer is sent by God into the world: "As the Father has sent me, so I send you" (John 20:21). Addressing the Father, Jesus says: "As you have sent me into the world, so I have sent them into the world" (John 17:18). Every man and woman is sent to proclaim the Resurrection in our time. In the author's words, "To speak about the resurrection is never an event only in the remote past or in distant future reality. It is best understood in the living community we call Church."

We live in the hope of seeing a "new heaven and a new earth" (Revelation 21:1), not in eternity, but already here on earth where we are faced with the same mystery of evil. And we repeat the sentence of Martha to Jesus: "Lord, if you had been here" (John 11:21), there would not have been all this evil, all these wars, all these merchants of death. But the Lord *is* here; we must return to the Jerusalem of the heart to find him and to believe that evil, despite all the reality to the contrary, does not have the last word. "Those who believe in me … will live" (John 11:25), says Jesus, and that person will triumph over evil.

We may consider one of the author's sentences to be the beginning of a response to the mystery of evil in the world: "The future has already begun." The future, which is the eternity of God – his light, triumph and the end of the present, which is an ongoing struggle. We are grateful to Fr. Rosica for his willingness to share his reflections that matured in the Holy Land and are now offered to all those who seek life in our time.

His Beatitude Michel Sabbah
Latin Patriarch-emeritus of Jerusalem

Jerusalem, September 14, 2017
Feast of the Exaltation of the Holy Cross

Preface

[The Resurrection] is part of the mystery of God that he acts so gently, that he only gradually builds up his history within the great history of mankind; that he becomes man and so can be overlooked by his contemporaries and by the decisive forces within history; that he suffers and dies and that, having risen again, he chooses to come to mankind only through the faith of the disciples to whom he reveals himself; that he continues to knock gently at the doors of our hearts and slowly opens our eyes if we open our doors to him. And yet – is not this the truly divine way? Not to overwhelm with external power, but to give freedom, to offer and elicit love. And if we really think about it, is it not what seems so small that is truly great?

Joseph Ratzinger – Benedict XVI
Jesus of Nazareth – Holy Week:
From the Entrance into Jerusalem to the Resurrection, p. 276

This little book came about in response to the very positive reception of my reflections on *The Seven Last Words of Christ*, published in 2017. Words or expressions uttered by Jesus on the cross lead us into a deeper relationship with the Lord who gave his life for us. With eyes of faith, we see beyond the humiliating death of Jesus of Nazareth and glimpse our God of mercy, redemption and enduring, endless love. But the tragic, violent events of Good Friday are not the end of the story. Death is not the final answer. This is the stunning proclamation or *kerygma* common to each evangelist: that God raised Jesus from the dead. He is the Lord of life! We have been saved by Jesus Christ! *Kerygma* (from the Greek *keryssein,* to proclaim, and *keryx,* herald) refers to the initial and essential proclamation of the Gospel message. The word appears nine times in the New Testament: once in Matthew (12:41), once in Mark (16:20), once in Luke (11:32), and six times in the letters of St. Paul (Romans 16:25; 1 Corinthians 1:21, 2:4, 15:14; 2 Timothy 4:17; and Titus 1:3). The *kerygma* is the very heart of the Gospel, the core message of the Christian faith that all believers are invited to proclaim. It is the duty of the Church to proclaim always and everywhere the Gospel of Jesus Christ, risen from the dead. To proclaim Jesus Christ, therefore, is the Church's mission. In his 1990 masterful encyclical letter *Redemptoris Missio, On the permanent validity of the Church's missionary mandate,* St. John Paul II emphasized how essential *kerygma* is in the life and mission of the Church:

Proclamation is the permanent priority of mission. The Church cannot elude Christ's explicit mandate, nor deprive men and women of the "Good News" about their being loved and saved by God. "Evangelization will always contain – as the foundation, center, and at the same time the summit of its dynamism – a clear proclamation that, in Jesus Christ … salvation is offered to all people, as a gift of God's grace and mercy." All forms of missionary activity are directed to this proclamation, which reveals and gives access to the mystery hidden for ages and made known in Christ (cf. Eph 3:3-9; Col 1:25-29), the mystery which lies at the heart of the Church's mission and life, as the hinge on which all evangelization turns.

… The subject of proclamation is Christ who was crucified, died, and is risen: through him is accomplished our full and authentic liberation from evil, sin and death; through him God bestows "new life" that is divine and eternal. This is the "Good News" which changes man and his history, and which all peoples have a right to hear (RM 44).

In another important section of St. John Paul II's encyclical letter, we read of the different emphases found in each evangelist's story of Jesus:

As for the different emphases found in each version, Mark presents mission as proclamation or kerygma: "Preach the Gospel" (Mk 16:15). His aim is to lead his readers to repeat Peter's profession of faith: "You are the Christ" (Mk 8:29), and to say with the Roman centurion who stood before the body of Jesus on the cross: "Truly this man was the Son of God!" (Mk 15:39). In Matthew, the missionary emphasis is placed on the foundation of the Church and on her teaching (cf. Mt 28:19-20; 16:18). According to him, the mandate shows that the proclamation of the Gospel must be completed by a specific ecclesial and sacramental catechesis. In Luke, mission is presented as witness (cf. Lk 24:48; Acts 1:8), centered especially on the Resurrection (cf. Acts 1:22). The missionary is invited to believe in the transforming power of the Gospel and to proclaim what Luke presents so well, that is, conversion to God's love and mercy, the experience of a complete liberation which goes to the root of all evil, namely sin.

John is the only Evangelist to speak explicitly of a "mandate," a word equivalent to "mission." He directly links the mission which Jesus entrusts to his disciples with the mission which he himself has received from the Father: "As the Father has sent me, even so I send you" (Jn 20:21). Addressing the Father, Jesus says: "As you sent me into the world, so I have sent them into the world" (Jn 17:18). The entire missionary sense of John's Gospel is expressed in the "priestly prayer": "This is eternal life, that they know you the only true God, and Jesus Christ whom you have sent" (Jn 17:3).

… The four Gospels therefore bear witness to a certain pluralism within the fundamental unity of the same mission, a pluralism which reflects different experiences and situations within the first Christian communities. It is also the result of the driving force of the Spirit himself; it encourages us to pay heed to the variety of missionary charisms and to the diversity of circumstances and peoples. Nevertheless, all the Evangelists stress that the mission of the disciples is to cooperate in the mission of Christ; "Lo, I am with you always, to the close of the age" (Mt 28:20). Mission, then, is based not on human abilities but on the power of the risen Lord. (RM 23)

There is no better place to appreciate these different emphases and Gospel pluralism than in our reflections on the Resurrection narratives. Not one of the evangelists recounts Jesus' Resurrection itself. It is an event taking place within the mystery of God between Jesus and the Father. By its very nature, the Resurrection event lies outside human experience. Several ambiguities and discrepancies between the Resurrection narratives of the New Testament raise some questions for us. When we encounter these questions and problems, there is almost an inevitable attempt to try to harmonize the stories of the Risen Lord and to tie together all the elements of the different Gospel accounts into a kind of historical reconstruction of our own imaginings. We must avoid this temptation at all costs and make the clear distinction between the basic *kerygma* and the unique ways that the accounts of the Risen Lord are handed on to us.

In the early Church, the Resurrection was not so much narrated or told but *proclaimed.* My reflections are not just a matter of relating stories and details of the past, but of truly proclaiming the Resurrection story anew in our day. What does it mean to proclaim the Resurrection in our day? It is not an attempt to answer the oft-asked question "What actually happened in the tomb on that first Easter morning?" This was not the preoccupation of the evangelists! What actually happened is that suddenly it became possible to know Jesus in the everyday of history (Mark); to live the Christian life within the community called Church (Matthew); to imitate Jesus in a meaningful life in our world (Luke); and to encounter Jesus in a deep, personal, loving, evolving relationship (John).

The details about the Risen Lord provided by each evangelist depended on the standpoint from which each Gospel writer chose to proclaim the Easter message, and on the particular historical moment in which he found himself. In proclaiming the Good News about Easter, the evangelist approached his effort with a set of questions, problems and difficulties that his own community was facing. This is the very reason why there are differences in the Gospel accounts of the Resurrection. We cannot preach the Good News of the Resurrection without taking into account the historical and theological situations of the evangelists and their communities.

Let us be very honest and admit that today, just as in the time of Luke writing in the Acts of the Apostles about the men and women of Athens, "[they] spend their time in nothing but telling or hearing something new" (Acts 17:21). Is it not true that many who hear about the Resurrection today respond to it as the people of Athens did back then? "When they heard of the resurrection of the dead, some scoffed; but others said, 'We will hear you again about this'" (Acts 17:32). What appeared to be a second chance offered to Paul of Tarsus to clarify matters was in reality a royal brushoff! In today's language, it could be something like "Yeah, right, heard that and done that!"

In our day, as in Paul's time, the Christian proclamation of Resurrection faith remains a stumbling block. Many who believe in the Resurrection of Jesus have often confused his Resurrection with the resuscitation of a dead body. They do not see the difference between God's raising his only son from the dead and Jesus' restoring Lazarus to ordinary life. The difference is clear: Lazarus had to die again. Jesus' life was not the same before and after his death. Jesus' life was totally transformed into a glorious existence that is now free from the limitations of space and time and is no longer subject to death. It is a reality difficult to fathom!

Our Christian faith in the Resurrection from the dead must never be taken for granted. Faced with the Risen Lord standing before us, our proclamation of his Resurrection must always be an invitation to Easter faith. Apart from our faith in the risen Christ, the Resurrection cannot be known. Both faith and the reality of the Resurrection in our lives are closely related to baptism, the great sacrament of Christian faith, in which "we have been buried" with Christ (Romans 6:4-5). Our baptism and the experience of our life as baptized Christians is the starting point of our proclamation. For this very reason, to speak about Resurrection is never an event only in the remote past or in distant future reality. It is best understood in the living community we call Church.

The core of my graduate studies in both Rome and Jerusalem was in the works of Luke – his Gospel and also his second volume that we know as the Acts of the Apostles. My thesis at the Pontifical Biblical Institute in Rome was on Luke's magnificent post-Resurrectional Emmaus story (24:13-35), and my research and writing at the École Biblique et Archéologique Française in Jerusalem was on Luke's rather exotic story of Philip and the Ethiopian eunuch (Acts 8:25-40). Spending several years immersed in those two stories gave me many new perspectives into the mystery of the Resurrection and helped me to know and love the Lord in a deeper way.

In the final analysis, the reality of the Resurrection will always remain acceptable and visible to the eyes of faith.

My greatest concern as a preacher and teacher of the Word of God these past 32 years of ordained ministry has been this: How can I give witness to the Resurrection in my own life? How can I make Resurrection faith more easily acceptable to contemporary women and men? How can I help others to encounter the Risen Lord and recognize him in the midst of our own shadows, despair and night? How can I help those who have no faith, who claim to be agnostics, atheists, skeptics or simply indifferent to the truth of Jesus, of the Gospels, or to the reality of eternal life. My only desire through these reflections is to present the living Lord who continues to meet us where we are, accompany us on our journeys, and cause our hearts to gradually catch fire within us along the way. Is not this what Pope Francis meant for the Church in the conclusion of his very moving address to the Bishops of the United States gathered in St. Matthew's Cathedral in Washington on September 23, 2015?

> Consequently, only a Church which can gather around the family fire remains able to attract others. And not any fire, but the one which blazed forth on Easter morn. The risen Lord continues to challenge the Church's pastors through the quiet plea of so many of our brothers and sisters: "Have you something to eat?" We need to recognize the Lord's voice, as the apostles did on the shore of the lake of Tiberius (Jn 21:4-12). It becomes even more urgent to grow in the certainty that the embers

of his presence, kindled in the fire of his passion, precede us and will never die out. Whenever this certainty weakens, we end up being caretakers of ash, and not guardians and dispensers of the true light and the warmth which causes our hearts to burn within us (Lk 24:32).

My sincere thanks to Joseph Sinasac and Simon Appolloni of Novalis Publishing in Canada for encouraging me to write this book. Once again, Anne Louise Mahoney's diligent eye and guidance helped bring the manuscript to completion. I thank the bishops, priests, women religious and lay women and men who took part in the many retreats I have led on the Resurrection narratives over the past years. Thanks to Francis Denis and Julian Paparella, competent and generous colleagues of the staff of Salt and Light Television, who assisted me with the preparation of these reflections. My deepest gratitude to His Beatitude Michel Sabbah, Latin Patriarch-emeritus of Jerusalem, for his generous Foreword to this book. He has been a mentor, guide, shepherd and friend to me since my years of study in Jerusalem – the blessed city that witnessed the Passion, suffering, death and Resurrection of the Lord. The Patriarch modelled for me what it means to be a witness to the Risen Lord today.

Fr. Thomas Rosica, CSB
Toronto, September 15, 2017
Feast of Our Lady of Sorrows

Introduction

Judaism has never been a monolithic religion. The Sadducees in the New Testament were of the priestly class – many of them were aristocratic, wealthy and theologically conservative. Scripture for them consisted only of the five books of Moses. No teaching was authoritative if it was not found in those books, called the Pentateuch, and they found no doctrine of the resurrection there. They baited Jesus with one of their classic "what if" questions, a question on which their minds had been settled long ago: there is no resurrection of the dead. They ridiculed the idea of the resurrection. Jesus rejects their naïve understanding of the resurrection (Luke 20:35-36) and then argues on behalf of the resurrection of the dead on the basis of the written law (20:37-38) that the Sadducees accept. There was no spirit of inquiry or desire to learn among them.

The Pharisees and many of the Lord's contemporaries hoped for the resurrection. They not only included the prophets and the writings in their Scripture, but also believed in the authority of the oral tradition from Moses.

The basis for belief in the resurrection was found in the oral tradition. The subject was heatedly debated between the Pharisees and Sadducees, a fact that Paul used to draw attention away from himself during his trial before the Jewish Council (Acts 23:6-10).

From the very beginning Christian faith in the resurrection has met with incomprehension and opposition. On no point does our faith encounter more opposition than on the resurrection of the body. St. Paul forcefully addressed the problem among the Corinthians: their denial of the resurrection of the dead (1 Corinthians 15:12) and their inability to imagine how any kind of bodily existence could be possible after death (15:35). Paul affirmed both the essential corporeity of the resurrection and its future orientation. His response moves through three steps: a recall of the basic *kerygma* about Jesus' Resurrection (15:1-11), an assertion of the logical inconsistencies involved in denying the resurrection of the dead (15:12-34), and an attempt to perceive theologically what the properties of the resurrected body must be (15:35-58).

Any denial of resurrection (15:12) involves logical inconsistencies. The basic one, stated twice (15:13, 16), is that if there is no such thing as (bodily) resurrection, then it has not taken place even in Christ's case. The consequences for the Corinthians were grave: both forgiveness of sins and salvation become an illusion, despite their strong convictions about both. Unless Christ is risen, their faith does not save. The question of the resurrection is vital and central not only to the Christian faith, but to all people who reflect on life and death.

The Resurrection and the Life

Immediately before his own death and Resurrection, Jesus proclaims: "I am the resurrection and the life" (John 11:25). The fourth-century Bishop Gregory of Nazianzus (328–389) spoke about the miracle in Bethany that prefigured Jesus' own death and Resurrection:

> He prays, but he hears prayer.
>
> He weeps, but he puts an end to tears.
>
> He asks where Lazarus was laid, for he was
>   a human being;
> and he raises Lazarus, for He is God.
>
> As a sheep he is led to the slaughter
> but he is the Shepherd of Israel and now of the
>   whole world.
>
> He is bruised and wounded,
> but he heals every disease and every infirmity.
>
> He is lifted up and nailed to the tree,
> but by the tree of life he restores us…
>
> He lays down his life,
> but he has the power to take it again;
>
> and the veil is rent, for the mysterious doors of
>   heaven are opened;
> the rocks are cleft, the dead rise.
>
> He dies, but he gives life, and his death destroys
>   death.
> He is buried, but he rises again.

The pathos-filled Gospel of the raising of Lazarus, the longest continuous narrative in John's Gospel (11:1-44) outside of the Passion account, is the climax of the signs of Jesus. The story is situated shortly before Jesus is captured, tried and crucified. It undoubtedly prefigures Jesus' own Resurrection from the dead. The Lazarus story is the event that most directly results in his condemnation by those seeking to kill him. The irony in John's Gospel is found in the fact that Jesus' gift of life leads to his own death. Jesus was aware of the illness of his friend Lazarus and yet he did not go to Bethany to work a miracle of healing of a sick person. In fact, he delayed for several days after Lazarus' death, meanwhile giving his disciples lessons along the way about the light – lessons incomprehensible in the face of grave illness and death, but understandable in the light shed by Lazarus' and Christ's resurrection.

Before the grave of his intimate friend Lazarus, Jesus declared to Martha, "I am the resurrection and the life. Those who believe in me, even though they die, he will live; and everyone who lives and believes in me will never die" (v. 25). And he adds, "Do you believe this?" (v. 26). The Lord urges us to respond just as Martha did: "Yes, Lord! We, too believe, despite our doubts and our darkness; we believe in you, because you have the words of eternal life; we want to believe in you, who gives us a trustworthy hope of life beyond life, of authentic and full life in your kingdom of light and peace."

Lord, if you had been here...

How often have we, like Martha and Mary, blurted out those same words of pain and despair: "Lord, if you had been here, my brother" … or sister or mother or father or friend … "would not have died" (v. 32). And this pathos-filled story from John's Gospel tells us what kind of God we have – a God who "groaned in spirit and was troubled." The Greek word used to describe Jesus' gut sentiment in verse 33 tells us that he became perturbed. It is a startling Greek phrase that literally means "He snorted in spirit," perhaps in anger at the presence of evil (death). We witness the Lord weeping at the tomb of his friend; a Saviour deeply moved at the commotion and grief of so many friends of Martha, Mary and Lazarus. The shortest line in the whole Bible is found in this Gospel story: "Jesus wept" (v. 35; New International Version).

Jesus reveals to us God who is one with us in suffering, grief and death… a God who weeps with us. God doesn't intervene to prevent the tragedies and sufferings of life. If we had a god who simply swooped down as some *deus ex machina* to prevent human tragedy and sinfulness, then religion and faith would be reduced to some form of magic or fate, and we would be helpless pawns on the chessboard of a whimsical god. Where is God in human tragedies? God is there in the midst of it all, weeping. This is our God who stands in deep human solidarity with us, and through the glory of the Incarnation, fully embraces our human condition.

Death of the heart and spirit

The story of the raising of Lazarus also speaks to us about another kind of death. We can be dead even before we die, while we are still in this life. This is not only the death of the soul caused by sin, but also rather a death that manifests itself through the absence of energy, hope, a desire to fight and to continue to live. We often refer to this reality as death of the heart or spiritual death. Many people are enchained in this kind of death every day because of the sad and tragic circumstances of their lives. People in these situations may not be able to do anything, not even pray. They are like Lazarus in the tomb. Jesus once spoke these words to his disciples: "Cure the sick, raise the dead" (Matthew 10:8). Among the corporal works of mercy – feeding the hungry; giving drink to the thirsty; clothing the naked; sheltering the homeless; visiting the sick; visiting prisoners – the last one he mentioned was to bury the dead. The provocative story of the raising of Lazarus tells us that in addition to this corporal work of mercy, we must also "raise the dead."

In the three cases of resurrection reported in the Gospels, all the successive physical aspects of death are mentioned. Jesus raised the daughter of Jairus when she was still lying on her bed (Mark 5:22-24, 35-43). He raised the son of the widow of Nain (Luke 7:11-17) while the boy was being carried out in a coffin. He raised Lazarus (John 11:1-44), who was already buried and decomposing. In each story, it is the compassion Jesus felt for the sorrowing relatives that was the primary cause of the miracle. When Jesus has compassion on the widow, saying, "Do not weep," he is not asking her to cheer up. Instead, it is a foreshadowing of his power. He will remove the cause of her tears and simultaneously give his disciples a preview of God wiping away all tears.

Yet after a certain period of time, the individuals raised from the dead returned to their former lives and would then eventually experience a final death. The miracle of a resuscitated corpse would indicate that Jesus' Resurrection was equivalent to the raising of the son of the widow of Nain, the daughter of Jairus, and Lazarus. Jesus' power to raise people from the dead is not dependent upon whether a person has just died, has been dead for days, or is already decomposing. Only the One who has entered death's realm and engaged death itself in battle can give life to those who have died. Jesus' power over death is absolute. Jesus rises from the dead, never to die again.

As Christians, we do not expect to escape death; we approach it with faith in the Resurrection. The raising of Lazarus is the prelude to what would come about after the horrific events of Good Friday in Jerusalem. The awesome events in Bethany were the prologue to what is described of each evangelist's Resurrection story in these pages, and prepare us to better understand Jesus' words to his grieving friends at the grave of Lazarus:

> "I am the resurrection and the life. Those who believe in me, even though they die, will live, and everyone who lives and believes in me will never die." (John 11:25)

1

Mark's Resurrection Account: A Call to Discipleship

Christians need to go out where Jesus is not known, or where Jesus is persecuted, or where Jesus is disfigured, to proclaim the true Gospel... To go out in order to proclaim. And, also, in this going out there is life, the life of the preacher is played out. He is not safe; there are no life insurance policies for preachers. And if a preacher seeks a life insurance policy, he is not a true preacher of the Gospel: He doesn't go out, he stays in place, safe. So, first of all: Go, go out. The Gospel, the proclamation of Jesus Christ, goes forth, always; on a journey, always. On a physical journey, on a spiritual journey, on a journey of suffering: we think of the proclamation of the Gospel that leads to so many wounded people – so many wounded people! – who offer their sufferings for the Church, for the Christians. But they always go out of themselves.

Excerpt of the Daily Homily of Pope Francis
Domus Sanctae Marthae, Vatican City
April 25, 2017

A s St. John Paul II pointed out in his encyclical letter *Redemptoris Missio*, the evangelist Mark presents mission as proclamation or *kerygma*: "Preach the Gospel" (Mark 16:15). His aim is to lead his readers to repeat Peter's profession of faith: "You are the Christ" (Mark 8:29), and to say with the Roman centurion who stood before the body of Jesus on the cross: "Truly this man was the Son of God!" (Mark 15:39) (RM 23).

Biblical scholars are almost universally agreed that Mark is the earliest Gospel, a fact that has serious implications for our understanding of the story of Jesus and how it was passed down to us from the beginning. The main problem with the Gospel of Mark for the final editors of the New Testament was that it appeared to be terribly deficient! In the first place, it is significantly shorter than the other Gospels – with only 16 chapters, compared to Matthew's 28, Luke's 24 and John's 20 and 21. We know nothing of Jesus' origins, according to Mark. There is a disproportionate emphasis on the Passion, suffering and death of Jesus. Even more significant is how Mark concludes it. The ending of this Gospel is strange! The Shorter Ending is found in 16:1-8. Mark 16:9-20, called the Longer Ending, has traditionally been accepted as a canonical part of the Gospel and was defined as such by the Council of Trent. Early citations of it by the Council Fathers indicate that it was composed by the second century, although vocabulary and style suggest that it was written by someone other than Mark. This ending is a general summary of the material concerning the appearances of the risen Jesus, reflecting, in particular, traditions found in Luke chapter 24 and John chapters 20 and 21.

A startling ending

In the earliest Gospel account of the Resurrection, found in Mark 16:1-8, the final scene is a startling one. The three women whom Mark named as having watched the crucifixion – two of whom also saw where the tomb was – buy spices as soon as the Sabbath is over, on Saturday evening after sunset. They go to the tomb at dawn the following morning, the first day of the workweek, expecting to have difficulty with the massive stone, and earnestly wishing that someone stronger will be around to help. It is an awesome, eerie, shocking scene. The women were not going to the tomb to witness Jesus' Resurrection! Such a thing was unthinkable. They were going to complete the Jewish burial ritual, a sad but necessary task both for respecting the body of the deceased and for covering over the smell of bodily decomposition. Other bodies would in due course be buried in the same tomb, prior to Jesus' bones being collected and put into an ossuary for the secondary entombment. Upon arriving at the garden tomb, the women got the shock of their lives. The stone was already rolled away! They found a young man, not an angel, who calmly explained to them that Jesus had been raised from the dead and would see them again in Galilee. The man told them:

"Do not be alarmed: you are looking for Jesus of Nazareth, who was crucified. He has been raised; he is not here. Look, there is the place they laid him. But go, tell his disciples and Peter that he is going ahead of you to Galilee; there you will see him, just as he told you." So they went out and fled from the tomb, for terror and amazement had seized them, and they said nothing to anyone, for they were afraid. (Mark 16:6-8)

The specific mention of Peter is not necessarily to give him a place of primacy among the apostles, but rather to stress that after his pitiful denials of his master and friend, Peter was not to be considered as one beyond redemption. The women were scared out of their wits and rushed home. They most likely passed several people on the way, but they didn't say a word. They were in shock!

This original ending of Mark's Gospel was viewed by later Christians as so deficient that not only was Mark placed second in the New Testament, but various endings were added by editors and copyists in some manuscripts that tried to soften this brutal, shocking ending and correct the story. The longest, most elaborate ending, which became Mark 16:9-19, was accepted by many Protestants and was included in the King James Version of the Bible, as well as in translations of the Latin Vulgate, used by Catholics. For countless millions of Christians over the centuries, the second ending became Sacred Scripture! Its authenticity is questionable, because it is not found in our earliest and most reliable Greek copies of Mark's Gospel. The language and style of the Greek is clearly not Markan, and the scribes and final editors most likely incorporated sections of the endings of Matthew, Luke and John to create a "proper" ending for Mark.

But the most striking aspect of Mark's ending is that we never encounter the Risen Lord! Is it possible that Mark's Gospel can really end with 16:8? What can we say about a resurrection story in which the risen Jesus himself never appears? How could Mark differ so much from Matthew's elaborate chapter 28 and Luke's masterful chapter 24; or John's highly developed portraits of the first witnesses of the Risen Lord in chapters 20 and 21?

The message of Mark's Gospel

Rather than dismiss the strangeness of Mark's ending, let us take stock of what Mark's Gospel offers us. Since Mark is our earliest account of Jesus' life, written (according to most scholars) around the time of the destruction of Jerusalem by the Romans in 70 AD, or shortly before that defining event, we have strong textual evidence that the first generation of Jesus' followers had no problem with a Gospel account that recounted no appearances of the Risen Jesus. We have to assume that the author of Mark's Gospel did not consider his account deficient in his transmission of the Jesus story and what he considered to be the authentic Good News about Jesus of Nazareth.

Is it not true that most preachers, pastoral ministers, catechists and Christians ignore Mark's account of the Resurrection? Since there is no mention of anyone encountering the Risen Lord, we don't allow Mark to have a voice in anything to do with the Resurrection of Jesus! On the other hand, if we allow Mark to speak to us as the first Gospel witness, we will learn something utterly amazing.

On the last night of Jesus' life in Mark's Gospel, he told his close friends, following their meal, "But after I am raised up, I will go before you to Galilee" (Mark 14:28). Mark believes that Jesus has been "lifted up" or "raised up" to the right hand of God, and the disciples would "see" him in Galilee. Mark believes that the disciples experienced appearances of and encounters with the Risen Jesus once they returned to Galilee after the eight-day Passover festival – and returned to their old fishing jobs in despair. This is what is related in the Gospel of Peter, one of the non-canonical gospels rejected as apocryphal by the Church Fathers and the Catholic Church's synods of Carthage and Rome, which formally established the New Testament canon. This Gospel of Peter, which had been carefully preserved in Egypt, was the first of the non-canonical gospels to be rediscovered. In that apocryphal text, Peter says:

> Now it was the final day of the Unleavened Bread; and many went out returning to their home since the feast was over. But we twelve disciples of the Lord were weeping and sorrowful; and each one,

sorrowful because of what had come to pass, departed to his home. But I, Simon Peter, and my brother Andrew, having taken our nets, went off to the sea. And there was with us Levi of Alphaeus whom the Lord ….

This same tradition shows up in an appended ending to the Gospel of John – chapter 21, where a group of disciples are portrayed back at their old fishing jobs on the Sea of Galilee. Also, Matthew knows the tradition of a strange encounter on a specific mountain in Galilee, where some of the eleven apostles doubt what they are actually seeing (Matthew 28:16-17)!

The Easter faith that Mark reflects, namely that Jesus has been "raised up" or lifted up to heaven, is similar to that mentioned by St. Paul, who is the earliest witness to Jesus' Resurrection in the 50s AD. Since Matthew, Luke and John come much later and clearly reflect the period after 70 AD when all of the first witnesses were dead – including Peter, Paul and James the brother of Jesus – they are clearly second-generation traditions.

Mark's is a very mysterious Gospel. Throughout his account, people are forever being told to remain silent; at the end of the story, the women do just that. Mark's Resurrection story contains an initial declaration and summary statement of all of Jesus' teaching in the Gospel: "Do not be alarmed" (16:6). The reader is told to abandon every fear. Second, the reader is told: "you are looking for

Jesus of Nazareth, who was crucified. He has been raised; he is not here. Look, there is the place they laid him" (16:6). Instead of a happily-ever-after conclusion, Mark offers us something far more powerful: a mysterious story that leaves us terribly unsettled, not content or with an attitude that we have it all figured out.

Mark proves to his hearers that Jesus was an authentic prophet and that his Passion predictions about his fate in Jerusalem would be realized. What is amazing is that Mark would abruptly end at the very point where he was about to tell us how the second part came true. He leaves us with profound questions: "What does this story mean for me? "What does it mean for the Church?" With eyes of faith and hearts sensitive to memory, we must go back to the beginning of Mark's story and rediscover what Mark stressed throughout his Gospel.

Jesus tried to teach the disciples that he would suffer, be killed and rise again from the dead. They didn't understand; they thought he was speaking in riddles. He certainly wasn't; he was speaking truthfully. Mark wants us to understand that fact. Jesus told the disciples, after the Transfiguration, that they were to tell no one about it "until after the Son of Man had risen from the dead" (9:9). They were in a conundrum, but Mark does not intend his readers to remain in a constant state of perplexity and bewilderment as to "what this rising from the dead could mean" (9:10).

Throughout all of Mark's Gospel, we are invited to view our lives in the shadow of the cross. Could it be that Jesus not only confirmed to his friends that he was indeed alive again in a new, though certainly bodily, way, but also commissioning them for the work that now awaited them (13:10; 14:9)? The ending may not have been very long, but it will have been important as the desired conclusion to the book, drawing the themes of this shocking Gospel to their proper conclusion. If Mark ended his Gospel where he did, might it be that he intended anyone reading the book out loud, as was done, to call on one of the eyewitnesses present in the community to tell the story of what they had witnessed in Jerusalem during the Passover celebrations, experienced on that Friday of infamy, endured on the frightful Saturday and experienced that first Easter day or shortly afterwards?

Questions for reflection

- How can I see the call to discipleship as the call to the cross?

- How does my personal story, with all its ups and downs, help me to preach the Jesus story?

- How does experiencing the power of God's mighty work and Jesus' Resurrection in daily life deepen my faith?

- When have I experienced such moments in my life?

- How can I proclaim this Good News in my words and actions?

2

Matthew's Resurrection Account: Fulfillment of the Promise to Be with Us

Marble floor

Our feet meet the earth in this place;
there are so many walls, so many colonnades,
yet we are not lost. If we find
meaning and oneness,
it is the floor that guides us. It joins the spaces
of this great edifice, and joins
the spaces within us,
who walk aware of our weakness and defeat.
Peter, you are the floor, that others
may walk over you (not knowing
where they go). You guide their steps
so that spaces can be one in their eyes,
and from them thought is born.
You want to serve their feet that pass
as rock serves the hooves of sheep.
The rock is a gigantic temple floor,
the cross a pasture.

This poem is from The Church, written in St. Peter's Basilica in Rome during the first session of the Second Vatican Council by then-Bishop Karol Wojtyla. He became Pope John Paul II in 1978.

Matthew tells the story of the Resurrection in four scenes: the women's experience at the tomb (28:1-7); their brief encounter with the Risen Lord (28:8-10); the Jewish leaders' attempt to deny and suppress the story (28:11-15); and the appearance to the disciples in Galilee (28:16-20). The final scene, ending with the Great Commission (28:19-20), is a programmatic conclusion to the entire Gospel.

For Matthew, the joy of the Resurrection overcomes all fear. On the first day of the week, two women went to the tomb: Mary of Magdala and Mary mother of James, also called "the other Mary." Suddenly the earth trembled and an angel appeared as lightning. The women present do not witness the Resurrection. They do, however, experience the earthquake, the appearance of the angel and the emptiness of the tomb – all of which are signs or traces of the divine activity that has brought these things about. We have heard the earthquake story once before. It is a sign of the decisive eschatological character of Jesus' Resurrection from the dead. At his death, the curtain of the Temple was torn in two, the earth shook, the rocks split and the tombs of the dead burst open (27:51-52). Matthew's use of these powerful signs and phenomena – earthquake, lightning angels announcing Jesus' victory over death – are told in apocalyptic language that was very common at that time. Apocalyptic language announces that the world had been finally transformed by the power of God! Jesus' breaking the bonds of death has cosmic and human resonances, which can be received only in faith.

The earthquake

Why is Matthew the only evangelist to have recorded the earthquake? How could it be that other evangelists did not write about this incredible miraculous phenomenon that caused many people to be raised from the dead and appear to the crowds in Jerusalem? Did Matthew make up this whole story? What effect might this have on belief in the physical Resurrection of Jesus from the dead? Let us recall that Matthew wrote his story of Jesus for a Jewish audience. Throughout his Gospel, Matthew stresses the fulfillment of Old Testament texts, to "fulfill what was spoken by the prophets (1:22-23; 2:15, 17, 23). The first recipients and readers of Matthew's story knew the Hebrew Scriptures!

Does Matthew mention the earthquake and the miraculous resurrection of many dead persons because the Jews, with the exception of the Sadducees, believed that people would physically rise from the dead? These Jews looked forward to a resurrection in the future. They knew what the ancient prophets like Daniel had written (12:2). Remember Jesus' conversation with Martha before her brother walked out of the tomb: "Your brother will rise again" (John 11:23). These words revealed Jewish belief of that time. Martha replied to Jesus: "I know that he will rise again in the resurrection on the last day" (11:24).

Nevertheless, Jesus anticipated that thought and raised his friend Lazarus several minutes later.

Most Jews of the first century believed in bodily resurrection, but they expected it to happen at the end of time. When Matthew spoke about the many people being raised from the dead immediately following Jesus' death, burial and Resurrection, it did not detract from the central message of his Gospel. The Jewish audience who first heard Matthew's story of Jesus would not have found the resurrection of many dead people to be a wild tale. They may have welcomed this thought and accepted it as a confirmation that Jesus was truly the great prophet and Messiah he claimed to be. Could this be why we are told that many priests came to believe in Jesus (Acts 6:7)? Perhaps the other Gospel writers, who directed their stories of Jesus to large Gentile audiences in a Hellenized world, wished to avoid the details and results of the earthquake to avoid distracting their communities from the centrality of Jesus' own glorious Resurrection from the dead.

Mark, Luke and John each describe Jesus raising at least one individual from the dead. Mark 5 and Luke 8 speak about the raising of the daughter of Jairus, and Luke 7 speaks of the raising of the son of a widow in the small village of Nain. John describes in great detail the raising of Jesus' friend Lazarus from the dead. Why would Mark, Luke and John bother to include these stories of the raising of people from the dead? Each of these accounts happened *before* Jesus' own Resurrection from the dead. This factor was a major difference. Jairus' daughter, the widow's son and Lazarus were not raised in their glorified bodies that would never die again. Jesus, on the other hand, did not have to endure the second death. He is the first fruit of those who rise from the dead (1 Corinthians 15:23).

Regarding Matthew's inclusion of the earthquake and subsequent resurrections of many from the dead, the bottom line is this: it is not simply a literary device added to this Gospel. The truth of Jesus' Resurrection from the dead does not depend on the veracity of the earthquake story (Matthew 27:51-53), nor does our Christian faith depend on it. Our faith is founded on the historical reality that Jesus died for our sins and conquered death when he rose from the dead on the third day. He offers that same glory to us. Nothing can change that reality or remove us from this central truth of our faith.

The women at the tomb were frightened, but the angel encouraged them, announcing Jesus' victory over death and sending them to go join the disciples of Jesus in Galilee. In Galilee they would be able to see him again. Galilee is the place where it all began. In the end, the disciples return to that mountain and are reconstituted as a community.

Then Jesus himself went to meet the women and said to them, "Rejoice!" And they fell on their knees and adored him in a seeming liturgical gesture. It is the stance of those who believe and accept the presence of God, even if it surprises and goes beyond the human capacity of understanding. Then Jesus himself orders them to go and join the brothers in Galilee: "Do not be afraid: go and tell my brothers to go to Galilee; there they will see me" (28:10).

The controversy around the tomb

Unlike Mark's and Luke's accounts, where the women come to bring spices to the tomb, Matthew draws our attention to the tomb itself. This is probably due to the fact that by the time this Gospel was written, the empty tomb had become an object of controversy. Matthew insists on the fact that it was the Jews themselves who had "a guard of soldiers and ... made the tomb secure by sealing the stone" (Matthew 27:65-66) and that the Jewish allegations were totally false (28:11-15). The guards who were guarding the tomb were so shaken up with fear that they were likened to dead men. The enemies, the chief priests of the Jews, defended themselves against the Good News of the Resurrection and sent word to say that the body had been stolen by Jesus' own disciples (28:11-13). The chief priests met and gave money to the guards. They were to spread the news that the disciples had stolen the body of Jesus to avoid everything that is said about the Resurrection because the chief priests did not accept the Good News of the Resurrection. They preferred to believe that it is an invention of the disciples of Jesus. To Matthew's contemporaries, the tomb was not just the "final resting place": it symbolized the power of death. Closed by a stone, it symbolized death's victory over life, but opened, it became a sign of victory over death, and the "angel of the Lord" who "rolled back the stone, and sat upon it is the sign of God's final victory over death."

The whole controversy over the tomb points to something much deeper than what is presented in this story. Such controversy continues in our own day! On the one hand, the effort of many persons to live and to witness to the Resurrection. On the other hand, so many evil people who fight against the Resurrection and against life.

Lessons of the women

There are significant lessons to be learned from the women who ran to the tomb that first Easter morning. They are witnesses of the death of Jesus (Matthew 27:54-56). At the moment of Jesus' burial, they remain sitting before the tomb, and therefore can testify to the place where Jesus was buried (Matthew 27:61). On Sunday morning, they are there once again. They know that the empty tomb is truly the tomb of Jesus! Their personal experiences of death and resurrection transformed their lives. They themselves become qualified witnesses of the Resurrection in the Christian communities. This is why they receive the order to announce, "Jesus is alive! He has risen from the dead!"

These women represented countless nameless yet devoted women who were part of the crowds Jesus addressed and in the homes he frequented. They were the courageous ones who reached out fearlessly to touch the fringe of his cloak. They shouted after him; they entered his hosts' houses uninvited; they poured expensive perfumed nard over his feet, to the consternation of the critics. They knew the promise made to them, they welcomed him, they knew from Jesus' own treatment of them the strength of their own testimony to him, and they were unafraid to show him great love. In the end, they stood beneath his dying body, while the men were hiding for fear of the authorities. It was the women who ground spices for his burial and calculated how to roll back the stone from his tomb. They attended firmly to the business of his living and dying. They were rewarded for their fidelity by being the first recipients of the Good News of the Resurrection.

Jesus' Great Commission

At the beginning of his Gospel, in presenting Jesus, Matthew says that Jesus is "Emmanuel, which means God is with us" (1:23). Now, at the end, the evangelist declares that Jesus is risen (28:6) and that he will be with us always, until the end of time! (28:20). In this final scene, Matthew literally makes Jesus present on the mountain where Jesus had directed the disciples to go (28:16-20). The evangelist points us back to the first programmatic sermon of Jesus on the mountain in Galilee (5:1–7:21). Matthew's meek and humble Jesus is the teacher as well as the example of meekness and humility. In revising and building on Mark's Gospel, Matthew deliberately completes the picture of Jesus and of the Christian life. The bleak image and invitation of the cross and the dead Jesus are filled out with a living and present Jesus whose words, founded upon the Scriptures of Israel, offer a consoling and learnable "way" to disciples willing to learn from him. Matthew issues the call to learn about the meek and humble Jesus. In perfect harmony with his presentation of Jesus, Matthew has chosen to end his Gospel not with a visual or pictorial representation of Jesus' new heavenly power, nor with sharing bread or touching his body, but with a profoundly simple scene featuring the words of Jesus, the great Teacher and Master (cf. 23:8-10). The Ascension scene is the goal to which the Gospel tends, and a rich synthesis of its fundamental message.

This final scene is divided into two parts: the appearance of the Risen Christ to the disciples in Galilee (28:16-18a), as promised in 28:7, and the instructions of Jesus, which conclude the Gospel (28:18b-20). The disciples go to the mountain as Jesus had commanded, a reminder of three earlier mountains: the mountain (5:1-2) where Jesus gave the Sermon on the Mount (Matthew 5–7); the high mountain (17:1) where he was transfigured (17:2) and his Passion prediction was ratified (16:21); and the Mount of Olives (24:3), the location of his eschatological discourse (24–25).

Let us consider for a moment the reality of this small group of apostles and disciples commissioned on the mountain in Galilee. Could any group of people be more human, more ordinary or less promising? How much more obvious could human frailty be than in this group – mired in treachery, cowardice and denial, to name but a few of the weak points of those who would become the "pillars" of our Church! Only when the one called "Rock" realized the full significance of his denial would the ministry of Church leadership and unity be placed on his shoulders. Two of them, James and John, displayed such naked ambition that they even included their mother in their attempts to secure their own glory (Matthew 20:20-21). Some would ask questions that clearly revealed their profound ignorance of the Master's message and life. Yet in the midst of such pathetic frailty and brokenness, Matthew's Gospel cuts through it all by telling us that "the eleven disciples" made their way to Galilee, "to the mountain to which Jesus had directed them" (28:16). No longer the Twelve – that symbolic number that gave them continuity with the long history of Judaism – but the eleven: recalling the tragic defection of Judas Iscariot who would fail most miserably. In spite of such blatant humanity and brazen failure, the eleven are entrusted with the dream and mission of the Risen Lord.

A universal mission

In verse 18, the Risen Jesus claims universal power in heaven and on earth. Since this universal power belongs to the Risen Lord, he gives the eleven a mission that is universal. They are to make disciples of *all* nations. While "all nations" is understood by some scholars as referring only to all Gentiles, it is probable that it included the Jews as well. Baptism is the means of entrance into the community of the Risen One: the Church. The end of Matthew's Gospel also contains the clearest expression in the New Testament of

Trinitarian belief. It may have been the baptismal formula of Matthew's church, but primarily it designates the effect of baptism, the union of the one baptized with the Father, Son and Holy Spirit.

In verse 20, Jesus' injunction "to obey everything that I have commanded you" refers certainly to the moral teaching found in Matthew's Gospel – pre-eminently that of the Sermon on the Mount (Matthew 5–7). The commandments of Jesus are the standard of Christian conduct; not the Mosaic Law as such, even though some of the Mosaic commandments have been invested with the authority of Jesus. The words "And remember, I am with you always, to the end of the age" (28:20) have a special ring to them. They send us back to the beginning of Matthew's account, when Jesus is given the name "Emmanuel" (1:23). In that name we find the answer to humanity's deepest longings for God throughout the ages. Emmanuel is both a prayer and plea (on our behalf) and a promise and declaration (on God's part). When we pronounce the word, we are really praying and pleading, "God, be with us!" And when God speaks it, the Almighty, Eternal, Omnipresent Creator of the world is telling us, "I am with you" in Jesus. At the conclusion of the Gospel, the name Emmanuel is alluded to when the Risen Jesus assures his disciples of his continued presence: "I am with you always, to the end of the age" (28:20). God did indeed keep his promise in Jesus.

The Eucharist confirms these words "I am with you." Christ said to his Apostles, "Go therefore and make disciples of all nations, baptizing them in the name of the Father and of the Son and of the Holy Spirit" (28:19). From Christ, the way of Christian initiation leads directly to the Eucharist: "I am with you. I am with every one of you. I become part of your flesh and blood. I share your very existence."

"Space travel of the heart"

In his book *Jesus of Nazareth – Holy Week: From the Entrance into Jerusalem to the Resurrection* (Ignatius Press, 2011), Pope Emeritus Benedict XVI writes of the mystery of the Ascension of the Lord:

> The old manner of human companionship and encounter is over. From now on we can touch Jesus only "with the Father." Now we can touch him only by ascending. From the Father's perspective, in his communion with the Father, he is accessible and close to us in a new way. This new accessibility presupposes a newness on our part as well. Through Baptism, our life is already hidden with Christ in God – in our current existence we are already "raised" with him at the Father's right hand (cf. Col 3:1–3).

> … At most we are far from him, but the path that joins us to one another is open. And this path is not a matter of space travel of a cosmic-geographical nature: it is the "space travel" of the heart, from the

dimension of self-enclosed isolation to the new dimension of world embracing divine love. (p. 286)

Questions for reflection

- Who is the Risen Jesus for me?

- From what fears do I need to be liberated?

- What earthquakes have I experienced in my life that have allowed me to encounter the powerful presence of God and his Son Jesus breaking through my history?

- How do I carry the good news of his Resurrection to others?

- From where can I draw the strength and courage I need to carry out my mission as a disciple of Jesus?

3

Luke's Resurrection Account: A Symphony in Three Movements

We are once again pilgrims on the road to Emmaus…
Our heads are bowed as we meet the Stranger
who draws near and comes with us.

As evening comes, we strain to make out His face
while he talks to us, to our hearts.

In interpreting the Book of Life,
He takes our broken hopes and kindles them
  into fire:
the way becomes lighter as,
drawing the embers together, we learn to fan
  the flame.

If we invite Him this evening,
He will sit down and together we shall share the meal.

And then all those who no longer believed will see
and the hour of Recognition will come.

He will break the bread of tears at the table of the poor
and each will receive manna to their fill.

We shall return to Jerusalem to proclaim aloud
what He has whispered in our ear.

And no doubt we shall find brothers and sisters there
who will greet us with the words:

"We too have met Him!"

For we know: the mercy of God has come to visit
the land of the living!

Brother Roger Schutz [1915–2005]
Prior of the Taizé Community

I consider the Resurrection chapter (24) of Luke's Gospel
to be a beautiful symphony in three major movements.
The first movement of this Easter symphony offers us
the empty tomb narrative (24:1-12): God alone breaks open
a helpless and hopeless situation. In the second movement,
the Emmaus story (24:13-35), God, in the person of Jesus,
accompanies people on their journeys through the ruins
of despair and death. The stories of the third movement
present Jesus among his disciples (24:36-53) and lead
people into an experience of community.

The First Movement:
A Hopeless Situation Reversed

Let us consider the first movement (24:1-12) of Luke's
Resurrection Symphony. The previous passage, recounting
the burial of Jesus (23:50-56), ends with a note that the
women who had come with Jesus from Galilee followed

Joseph of Arimathea and saw the tomb and how the body of Jesus was laid. The women knew the exact tomb where Jesus was placed. There was no possibility of mistaking it. Having prepared spices and ointments, they rested on the Sabbath according to the Jewish law. As soon as the Sabbath was over, they came to embalm the body of Jesus for proper burial. It is the women who first discover the empty tomb and receive the message of the angels that Jesus has been raised. While the women are not named in Chapter 23, in 24:10 we learn that it was Mary Magdalene, Joanna, the mother of James, and some others. Even though the Apostles were to be witnesses to the Resurrection (Acts 1:22), they seem to be in disarray, while the women disciples are on hand to receive the joyful news.

In their great perplexity before the empty tomb, the women are asked why they seek the living one among the dead. They are challenged by the two men in dazzling clothes to remember what Jesus had told them while he was still in Galilee, that the Son of Man had to suffer, be crucified, and on the third day rise again. In one brief moment, everything changes! Jesus "is not here, but has risen" (Luke 24:5). God breaks open a helpless and hopeless situation.

Remembering Jesus' words

The four Gospels were written from the perspective of the faith of the disciples after they experienced the actual events of Jesus' death and Resurrection. Throughout these stories, there is a dynamic interplay between event, faith and the final shape of the biblical text. There is repeated admonition to remember words and events from the past. In fact, one of the human pitfalls or flaws is that we too quickly forget what God had said or done. God, on the other hand, does not forget. God remembers and is faithful to his word and covenant. In verse 8 of chapter 24 we read, "Then they remembered his words." The women respond in faith by remembering the words of Jesus. They believe the message of the angels by remembering what Jesus said, and they go to tell the eleven and the others the Good News. But their words "seemed to them an idle tale, and they did not believe them" (24:11). The women believe, but the eleven Apostles do not!

While Luke gives much prominence to the Apostles, both in his Gospel and in Acts, he also points out the failure of human leaders in the story. Some feel that the Apostles did not believe the women because they were women! They say that things might have been different had the first witnesses at the tomb been men. I do not think that the problem was due to the fact that women were involved as witnesses at the tomb. The much deeper issue is that the male apostles did not remember what Jesus had told them. Despite the men's disbelief, Peter apparently believed the women enough to run to the tomb, where he saw the linen cloths, and then went home amazed at what had happened. His response is hardly genuine faith. Amazement falls short of authentic faith. The crowds who saw the miracles of Jesus could be amazed but still not become disciples. They remained disbelieving. Discipleship requires commitment, trust and obedience; amazement does not.

The Second Movement: Accompaniment on the Road

The best-known section of chapter 24 is found in the second movement of Luke's Resurrection Symphony: the beloved story of the Road to Emmaus that begins at verse 13. It serves as a transition between the events of the Passion and discovery of the tomb and the appearance tradition. It is different from the other Resurrection appearances because the Lord disappears at the moment of recognition. The narrative (24:13-35) serves as a bridge between the empty tomb (24:1-12) and Jesus' self-revelation to his apostles (24:36ff.) immediately following the Emmaus disciples' meal, their recognition of Jesus and their hasty return to Jerusalem.

The Emmaus episode must be read in light of the inaugural scene of Jesus' ministry in Luke's Gospel in the Nazareth synagogue (4:16-30). There Jesus sets forth his universal mission repeating the words of the prophet Isaiah (61:1-2). After he outlines the major points of his ministry in this programmatic scene, the crowd grows terribly envious of one of their own and tries to get rid of him. Initially, Jesus' words get a warm reception, but then murmuring and doubts begin to arise, to the point that the initial wonder and awe at his words turn into indignation and hostility. The people of Nazareth refused to hear his

central message of liberation, freedom and reconciliation; they heard an approximation of it, highly coloured
by their own attitudes. Jesus did not succeed in making
himself heard and understood; he had to depart in haste
… for his life (4:30). The first images of the ministry of
Jesus that the evangelist Luke gives to the audience are
of a man who is defeated, unheeded and unwelcomed. If
Jesus is the evangelist par excellence, how could he begin
his ministry in such a manner? He seems to be a failed
evangelist from the start!

Jesus' vindication as a successful evangelist happens
only at the end of Luke's Gospel, on the road to Emmaus.
This story continues the great theme of "the journey" that
began in Luke 9:51 and does not end with the death of
the Messiah. Emmaus is a continuation of Jesus' journey,
his pursuit of wayward disciples that was prefigured by
the parable of the shepherd who went in search of lost
sheep until he found them and returned them to the fold
(15:3-7). Without being aware of what they are saying, the
two disciples on the road profess the central elements of
the creed of the Christian faith (except for references to
the Resurrection, the Ascension and return in glory), but
remain blind to the necessity of the Messianic suffering predicted in the Scriptures. The irony of the situation is obvious: Cleopas and his unnamed companion are announcing
the message of salvation as if it were a misfortune! After
Jesus challenges them to reinterpret the events of the past
days in light of the Scriptures, they share a meal together.

After breaking the bread with them, he disappears and their eyes are finally opened. On the road, their hearts gradually began to burn as they come to understand with their minds the truth about the suffering Messiah. At table in Emmaus, they recognize Jesus in the breaking of the bread.

Let us consider each moment of this symbolic Resurrection story and discover how each expression and movement echoes in our own lives.

The identity of the unnamed disciple

For centuries it was believed and frequently portrayed that the unnamed disciple walking on the road to Emmaus was a man. Surely one of them was male and his name was Cleopas (Luke 24:18). Unlike the fidelity and perseverance of the beloved disciple and the unnamed woman in John's Gospel, the Lukan companion of Cleopas may very well be an example of one who fled because of fear, despair and lack of faith in the promises of the Lord Jesus and the words of the Scriptures. Even in that flight back to their previous ways of life and thinking, the Risen Lord heals, encourages, removes blindness, fear and doubt, and restores his followers to just and loving relationships with God, with himself and with the community of believers.

Nevertheless, the identity of this unnamed person has intrigued me. Why did Luke choose not to name this person? Does this suggest that the first hearers and readers of the Gospel would have known the identity of the unnamed figure? Was it Luke? Peter? or perhaps the wife of Cleopas?

Since the time of Origen, attempts have been made to iden-tify the companion of Cleopas as Peter. But this is unlikely in view of verse 34. For Luke, the companion is unnamed, which raises the question of why he names Cleopas. I sug-gest that Luke might be designating Cleopas' unnamed companion as a "type" of Christian disciple. Could the identity of this unnamed person be the result of conflated identities of "Mary the mother of James" (Matthew 27:56; Mark 15:40, 16:1; Luke 24:10), present at the Crucifixion and a witness of the empty tomb, and "Mary the wife of Clopas" (John 19:25), also present at the Crucifixion? "Clopas" seems to be a variant spelling of "Cleopas." I like to imagine this unnamed figure as the wife of Cleopas. If his wife, Mary, was in Jerusalem for Passover, it makes sense that she would travel back home to Emmaus, or at least stop there on her way home with her husband. It wouldn't have been unusual for a married couple to privately carry on a conversation with each other along the way, sharing about the traumatic experience they had just endured in Jerusalem – their mentor and friend they had followed these past years, dead, and now said to have risen. What could this mean for them and for their future?

In the midst of their intense, grief-laden conversation on the road, this stranger catches up with them and shares his understanding of the things that had just happened in Jerusalem. They were unable to recognize him because they were so bewildered and wrapped up in their own grief. Jesus accompanied the couple and led them from blindness to sight. As soon as they recognize him after the bread is broken, he disappears from their midst. They are both able to look back over the past few hours and see how Jesus slowly brought them back to faith (v. 32) and helped them discover the meaning of the Messiah's suffering, death and Resurrection.

Cleopas and his wife slowly journeyed through the darkness and desperation of faith. They had to discover anew God's Word and God's Envoy: the Risen Lord. Their initial sadness, non-understanding and disbelief are transformed into joy as they eagerly listened to the explanation of the Scriptures on the road, and as their eyes were opened at table in Emmaus. They found new meaning in the breaking open of the Scriptures and the sharing of bread. Such a discovery produces a desire in them to return to the assembled community in Jerusalem, and to share with those who waited there the good news of the Resurrection.

"We had hoped…"

Without being aware of what they are really saying along the road, Cleopas and his wife profess many of the central elements of the creed of the Christian faith, but they remain blind to the necessity of the Messianic suffering predicted in the Scriptures. The Emmaus disciples saw their hopes and dreams crushed with the brutal death of their Lord and Master. Theirs is a heart-wrenching cry: "We had hoped" (24:21). They were expecting this Jesus to be a mighty liberator or warrior. They never imagined the outcome of that terrible Friday on a hill outside the walls of Jerusalem.

They know lots of facts about Jesus, but are unable to bring them together and realize that he is walking with them! They are unable to connect the dots. The stranger on the road to Emmaus takes the skepticism and curiosity of the disciples and weaves them into the fabric of the Scripture. Jesus challenges them to reinterpret the events of the past days in light of the Scriptures, and they share a meal together.

We know only too well what happens when such experiences overtake us: we become despondent, indifferent, cynical and sad. How many times have we been like the two disciples on the road, uttering those same words – "We had hoped"? *We had hoped that the marriage would remain intact and the family united. We had hoped that wars, violence and terrorism would have ceased. We had hoped that the economic crisis would not affect our family, resulting in job loss, uncertainty and imposed poverty. We had hoped that our children would remain in the Church. We had hoped that the ravages of sickness and aging would spare a loved one or even ourselves much physical and mental anguish.* Like the two on the road to Emmaus, do we not feel that we are often victims of time, fate, circumstance and uncontrollable external factors? Jesus does not want his disciples to simply recite a shopping list of nice expressions of hope. He wants them to *be* hope. We cannot afford to simply be people who had hoped. Rather, we must *become* hope, and we can be so only if we remain united to Jesus.

"Stay with us"

Nightfall at Emmaus is not only the sunset of that first Easter: it marks the night of faith and doubt, uncertainty and obscurity, confusion and chaos. "Stay with us, because it is almost evening" (24:29). This was the fervent plea that the two disciples addressed to the stranger who had walked with them along the way. "Stay with us" is also the prayer of the early Church to the Risen Lord that he not abandon them in their searching for his new presence. At table in Emmaus, the disciples' hearts began to gradually burn within them (24:32) as they came to understand with their minds the truth about the suffering Messiah. The "Good News" descended from their head to their heart, and they experienced that strange and wonderful feeling of their hearts gradually becoming on fire. This is the only way for them to adequately describe their recognition of the Lord.

Pounding and burning hearts

The Emmaus story helps us realize that believing is not a matter of the mind, but a matter of the heart. It will only be with pounding and burning hearts that we come to believe. What we believe is what we give our heart to. Resurrection is not a *head* trip, but a *heart* trip. In the intimacy of the breaking of the bread, the disciples' eyes opened and they recognized the Risen One in their midst.

Then Jesus disappears! He had kindled a fire in the hearts of those who travelled with him.

We often translate the expression of the two disciples at table in Emmaus as "Were not our hearts burning within us," but the Greek text uses a perfect present participle that includes the connotation of a gradual warming of the heart as he spoke to them on the road and opened for them the meaning of the Scriptures. I have translated the disciples' words like this: "Were not our hearts *gradually* catching fire within us…?" The verb means burning, or to be slowly burning. I find that this "gradual" burning of the heart is in harmony with the whole journey of Cleopas and his wife, of their coming to faith and their understanding the events of salvation history in a completely new way. How fitting are the words of François Mauriac, the French Catholic author of the last century: "If you are friends with Christ many others will warm themselves at your fire. On the day when you no longer burn with love, many will die of the cold."

Appearance to Simon

Just as the two disciples were moving away from the city of Jerusalem in verse 13, the end of the story finds them moving back to Jerusalem to be reunited with the other disciples and Apostles who waited for Jesus in the Holy City (24:33). The story's conclusion is an abrupt announcement by the assembly to the ones returning to the community rather than, as expected, the two disciples' relating what they had just experienced (24:33-34). How can we describe the Lord's appearance to Peter and the group of Apostles and disciples in Jerusalem? Does Luke have the "eleven and their company" proclaim the appearance to Peter and announce it before the travellers' report to be true to the Lucan understanding of the apostolic circle around Peter as first "witness with us to his resurrection" (Acts 1:22)? The appearance to Peter and the testimony of the Apostles thus obtain logical priority in the building of the Church. From the very beginning, there was great significance attached to "being with Peter and the apostolic circle." This does not diminish the Emmaus travellers' encounter. On the contrary, the happening "on the road" is authenticated and confirmed by being made part of the greater, unified Easter witness of the assembly of apostles and disciples of Jesus.

Nostalgia

At the end of this second movement of the Resurrection Symphony, the question lingers: Why does Luke alone spend so much time relating the Emmaus event? The story was most likely told in response to Jesus' continuing historical absence and its perception as a loss to Jesus' followers. The main theme of the second movement of the Resurrection Symphony is truly recognition of the Lord, not just of his bodily presence, but of his powerful presence in the Scriptures and in the breaking of the bread. The main issue is how Luke uses the story to teach his readers in 80 AD. They might have been saying to themselves how fortunate people were 50 to 60 years earlier to have seen the Risen Lord with their own eyes. Nostalgia would cause people to say that having been there back then might make a difference in the way they think and believe today! But Luke says that even those who were there weren't able to recognize Jesus until the Scriptures were "opened" and the Eucharistic meal was shared. The bottom line is this: a past generation is not more fortunate or blessed to have encountered the Risen Jesus than a generation that hasn't seen him. Faith in Jesus transcends all history, space and time. Christians of Luke's time and Christians of our time have the same essential elements for recognizing the Lord: Sacred Scripture and the Eucharist.

For Cleopas and his wife on that first Easter, their journey was a gradual, painstaking process requiring a careful remembering and rearticulation of the events of salvation history found in the Scriptures, along with an experience of the Risen Lord. It is no less the same for twenty-first century Christians who continue to interpret the Scriptures in this day and age, and move from faith-filled insights to a proclamation and lived experience of the One who is truly risen from the dead.

The Third Movement: Eating and Drinking with Jesus

Table fellowship reveals the depth of our humanity. The touching human scene of Jesus taking bread and fish and eating it with his disciples drives home the fact that ghosts don't eat – humans do – and reassures the disciples that the Risen Lord is truly in their midst (24:36-50).

This movement parallels John 21 with the subject of the cooked fish. In John 21:9-14, Jesus was cooking the fish. In Luke, the disciples gave Jesus the cooked fish to eat. If Luke 13:35-48 is combined with the narrative from the Road to Emmaus (Luke 24:13-35), both stories involved the breaking of bread (Luke 24:30, 35 and John 21:13). The most notable narratives with the blessing of bread and fish were the multiplication of the loaves and fishes (Mark 6:30-44, 8:1-9; Matthew 14:13-21, Matthew 15:32-39; Luke 9:10-17; John 6:1-14). A meal that featured fish and bread was common around the Sea of Galilee and in Jerusalem. Such meals were a regular part of life on the road with Jesus and his followers.

The striking humanity of Jesus at table finally convinces the Emmaus disciples that he is alive. Despite the testimony from the women and the two travellers, the disciples still could not believe their eyes when Jesus appeared before them. Like the appearance to Thomas in John's Gospel, Jesus showed his followers his hands and feet (not his hands and side). It was necessary to touch the Risen Lord. Unlike a ghost, Jesus has substance.

It is often the ordinary moments of table fellowship that bring about the realization that we are human – loving, loveable and genuinely interested in others, in their tribulations, their hopes and their futures. Table fellowship reveals the depth of humanity and the depth of compassion. It is a springboard to adult faith and to a living encounter with the Risen Lord who wishes to share his own life with us each day.

In Jesus, the Future Has Begun

Just as Jerusalem was the city of destiny in the Gospel of Luke (the place where salvation was accomplished), Jerusalem occupies a central position at the beginning of the Acts of the Apostles. It is the starting point for the mission of the Christian disciples to "the ends of the earth," the place where the Apostles were situated and the doctrinal focal point in the early days of the community (Acts 15:2, 6).

The first verses of the Acts of the Apostles (Acts 1:1-2) connect the book of Acts with the Gospel of Luke, and show that the Apostles were instructed by the Risen Jesus (1:3-5). The disciples were anxious for answers. They asked, "Lord, is this the time when you will restore the kingdom to Israel?" (1:6). They thought "the promise of the Father" (1:4) would bring about an age of political sovereignty such as the nation had enjoyed under the reign of King David. But Jesus' answer made clear that this is not what the promise is all about. Neither would the promise give them a glimpse of the end times, for "It is not for you to know the times or periods that the Father has set" for the end of time (1:7). The promise was not going to make their lives easier by restoring political or national dominance or by granting divine insight. When they received the Spirit, they too would be baptized in fire. They would be empowered to take on the role of Christ: to teach, to nourish and to serve; to be ignored, to suffer and to die for him.

After speaking, Jesus was lifted up into the heavens before his friends. Just imagine this awesome scene! How did it feel to them to watch their Lord and Master leave? The angels' words to the "men of Galilee" are painfully blunt and leave little room for misinterpretation: "Why do you stand looking up toward heaven? This Jesus, who has been taken up from you into heaven, will come in the same way as you saw him go into heaven" (1:11).

The disciples are given a last bit of instruction: "Don't keep trying to stare into the future. Don't be overly concerned about at which hour he will come back." We, too, must not stand idly staring up into the heavens and moaning about the past, about which we can do nothing, except to bury it deeply in God's hands and heart. The Lord will be glorified, and it follows that his disciples will also share in his glory. Let's get going and carry a piece of heaven into the world. This is the meaning of the Resurrection and the Ascension of our Lord – not divine abandonment of the human cause, but divine empowerment of the Gospel dream!

Conformity to the Scriptures

Luke's Gospel ends as it began (1:9): in the Jerusalem temple (24:53). The final scene emphasizes that what is written in the Jewish Scriptures must necessarily be fulfilled because it reveals the plan of God, which never fails to be accomplished. The life, death and Resurrection of Christ are fully in accord with the Scriptures. The clearest expression of this is found in the words addressed by the

Risen Christ to his disciples: "These are my words that I spoke to you while I was still with you – that everything written about me in the law of Moses, the prophets, and the psalms must be fulfilled" (24:44). This statement shows the basis of the necessity for the Paschal mystery of Jesus, affirmed in numerous passages in the Gospels: "The Son of Man must undergo great suffering … and on the third day be raised" (Luke 9:22); "But how then would the scriptures be fulfilled, which say it must happen in this way?" (Matthew 26:54); "this scripture must be fulfilled in me" (Luke 22:37).

Through his Ascension, Jesus shows that clinging to him in time and history serves no purpose. Nor does he cling to the human beings around him: he lets them go free so they can continue their Gospel mission. His whole life, death and Resurrection teach us to accept everyone and everything as a gift, on loan to us. Only in his physical separation from the historical scene can his spiritual union with the entire world – for all time – be complete. Jesus left the world one day in order to be available to all people throughout all time. He had to dissolve bonds he had made with his friends to be available for everybody. In Jesus, the future has already begun! In the words of St. John Chrysostom: "He whom you love is no longer where he was before. He is now wherever you are."

Questions for reflection

- When have I found myself before stone walls or tombs, when nothing or no one could revive my hopes or alleviate my despair?

- When have I taken the road back to Emmaus, preferring to remain in the familiar, among what is known and calculable, rather than move forward to the unknown challenges of new life?

- How is Jesus alive and present among us? Is my own friendship with him contagious?

- When have I experienced that strange and wonderful feeling of "the burning heart" as I listened to the Word of God at the Eucharist or in private prayer?

- How have certain events helped me to refine and rethink my proclamation of the Good News?

4

John's Resurrection Account: Meeting a God of Love and Mercy

The wounds of Jesus are a scandal, a stumbling block for faith, yet they are also the test of faith. … Saint John XXIII and Saint John Paul II were not afraid to look upon the wounds of Jesus, to touch his torn hands and his pierced side. … These were two men of courage, filled with the parrhesia of the Holy Spirit, and they bore witness before the Church and the world to God's goodness and mercy….

In these two men, who looked upon the wounds of Christ and bore witness to his mercy, there dwelt a living hope and an indescribable and glorious joy (1 Pet 1:3,8). … The hope and joy of Easter, forged in the crucible of self-denial, self-emptying, utter identification with sinners, even to the point of disgust at the bitterness of that chalice. Such were the hope and the joy which these two holy popes had received as a gift from the risen Lord and which they in turn bestowed in abundance upon the People of God, meriting our eternal gratitude.

Excerpt of the Homily of Pope Francis, Mass of Canonization of Blesseds John XXIII and John Paul II
St. Peter's Square, April 27, 2014

John's Resurrection account tells of appearances of the Risen Lord in both Jerusalem and Galilee. The Resurrection stories of the fourth Gospel are a series of encounters between Jesus and his followers that reveal diverse faith reactions. Whether these encounters are with Simon Peter and the Beloved Disciple, Mary Magdalene, the disciples, or Thomas, the whole scenario reminds us that in the vast range of belief are various degrees of readiness and different factors that cause people to come to faith.

The Morning Race to the Tomb (John 20:3-5)

One of my favorite paintings is *The Disciples Peter and John Running to the Tomb on the Morning of the Resurrection* by the well-known Swiss painter Eugène Burnand (1850–1921). Each time I look at this remarkable masterpiece, displayed in the Musée d'Orsay in Paris, I am caught up in the movement of the beloved disciple who clasps his hands in prayer, while Peter holds his hand over his heart. We can easily feel the rush as their hair and cloaks are lifted by the early morning breeze. Burnand's depiction of the Resurrection is not frozen in time, static, without emotion, but is utterly dynamic, forward-looking, filled with deep feeling. The artist captured beautifully the moment presented by John the evangelist.

John outran Peter to the garden where the tomb was located. As soon as he arrived, John 20:5 tells us, "He bent down to look in and saw the linen wrappings lying there, but he did not go in." The Greek word for "bent down" means "to peer into; to peep into; to bend low to take a closer look; to stoop down to see something better." John bent down so he could peek into the tomb, and he "saw the linen wrappings lying there." The Greek word for "linen wrappings" is the identical word used in John 19:40 in reference to the shroud in which Joseph of Arimathea and Nicodemus had buried Jesus. If the body of Jesus had been stolen, whoever took him would have taken this expensive garment as well, but John saw that these linen clothes had been left lying in the tomb. John's Gospel account also mentions a peculiar detail about the facial cloth that was "rolled up in a place by itself." The word in Greek means "to neatly fold; to nicely arrange; or to arrange in an orderly fashion." Could this be an indication that Jesus was calm and completely in control of his faculties and mobility when he was raised from the dead? Did he neatly fold the facial cloth and carefully place it to one side, separate from the linen wrappings? Unlike Lazarus, who emerges from the darkness of the tomb and needs to be unbound and set free by others, Jesus is in control of his situation and needs no assistance.

Given John's penchant for symbolism, many people have tried to decipher the possible symbolic message encoded in this early morning race of Peter and the Beloved Disciple to the tomb. Is it simply a question of the Beloved Disciple being younger and more agile than Peter? Or could it be that these two apostolic figures represent two currents, streams or trends within the early Church, and perhaps a tension within the Johannine community – with Peter representing the more staid, traditional, authority-minded model, and the Beloved Disciple representing the more charismatic, Spirit-filled, enthusiastic, less institutional model that may have existed in John's community?

Was the Beloved Disciple considered the origin of a movement that claimed deeper spiritual insights into Jesus' identity, which were perhaps set aside in the beginning by the more mainline communities? Perhaps the Beloved Disciple arriving first signifies the emotional rush of those guided by their hearts and their personal experience of Jesus, but the fact that he waits outside and allows Peter to enter first suggests a certain deference for the Church's duly appointed leadership. Closer to Jesus both in life (13:23) and in death (19:26-27), the Beloved Disciple sees the significance of the garments left behind in the empty tomb, while Peter does not notice them (20:8-10). The disciple who was bound closest in love to Jesus was the fastest to look for him, and the first to believe in him. But what did he believe? John does not tell us. He simply believed, and without another word exchanged, he and Peter returned to their homes.

We also know from John 20:11 that Mary Magdalene soon followed Peter and John back to the tomb, for she was present at the site and remained there after Peter and John returned to the other Apostles, who were locked in a room for fear of the authorities. By the time the women reached the Apostles, they must have sounded very confused. The Apostles didn't take the women seriously. They thought the women were telling idle tales – in Greek, nonsense, babble, or delirium. Who did these women think removed Jesus from the tomb? Which story was true? Was Jesus resurrected and alive, as the women had said, or had his body been stolen?

The rest of the story belongs to Mary. She is the one who saw the angels. She is the one who saw the Risen Lord. Peter and the beloved disciple saw nothing but a vacant tomb with two piles of clothes in it. They saw nothing but emptiness and absence, and on that basis at least one of them believed, although neither of them fully understood what had happened.

Mary Magdalene, Mary of Bethany (sister of Martha and Lazarus) and the unnamed penitent woman who anointed Jesus' feet (see Luke 7:36-48) are sometimes understood to be the same woman. From this, plus the statement in Luke's Gospel that Jesus had cast seven demons out of Mary Magdalene, has arisen the view that she had been a prostitute. In reality, we know nothing about her sins or weaknesses. They could have been inexplicable physical disease, mental illness, or anything that prevented her from wholeness in mind and body. Mary Magdalene is mentioned in the Gospels as being among the women of Galilee who followed Jesus and his disciples. She was also present at his crucifixion and burial, and went to the tomb on Easter Sunday to anoint his body.

In John's very moving intimate Easter Gospel, we peer into the early morning scene of sadness as Mary Magdalene weeps uncontrollably at the grave of her friend Jesus. John does not tell us when Mary arrived at Jesus' burial place (20:11-18). She is simply there, and the emphasis is on her tears and her uncontrollable grief. When Mary bends down to look in the tomb, she sees the angels. They are sitting, presumably on the ledge of the burial place, at the two ends of the grave clothes, where Jesus' body had been.

In the Scriptures, when someone encounters an angel, that person is frequently overcome with terror and fear. John does not mention any such feeling on Mary's part. Realizing her sadness and grief, the angels do not startle her with good news, but ask the question that can allow her to name her grief and find healing. The angels say to her with great compassion, "Woman, why are you weeping?" (v. 13). This is in striking contrast with their triumphant announcement of the Resurrection recorded in the other Gospel accounts of the empty tomb (Matthew 28:5-7; Mark 16:6-7; Luke 24:5-7).

Mary's answer (v. 13) shows that she is totally focused on the fact that Jesus' body is missing. He is still her Lord even though he is dead; her loyalty is to him. When she tells the angels that she does not know "where they have put him," she may be thinking that Joseph of Arimathea or his friends may have moved Jesus to a more permanent grave. Her answer allows the angels to truly announce to Mary the Good News, but they are interrupted by the sudden appearance of the Risen Lord!

Mary saw him, but did not realize it was Jesus (v. 14). Her own deep sadness and grief prevented her from linking together all the details: the grave clothes, the presence of angels, the absence of the body. The very object of her concern – Jesus – stands before her, but she is blinded from recognizing him. Deep emotions have this effect on us. Mary's inability to recognize him seems to be attributed to the nature of Jesus' resurrection body, since such failure is typical of encounters with him (cf. Matthew 28:17; Mark 16:12; Luke 24:16, 37; John 21:4).

When Jesus calls her by name, she turns and says to him in Hebrew,

> "Rabbouni!" (which means Teacher). ... [Jesus says] "Do not hold on to me, because I have not yet ascended to the Father. But go to my brothers and say to them, 'I am ascending to my Father and your Father, to my God and your God.'" Mary Magdalene went and announced to the disciples, "I have seen the Lord"; and she told him that he had said these things to her. (John 20:15-18)

Mary's was a seemingly short journey with earth-shattering ramifications. Because of her incredible message and mission, she was fittingly called *Apostola Apostolorum* (Apostle to the Apostles) in the early Church because she was the first to see the Risen Lord and to announce his Resurrection to the other apostles.

Jesus lived in an androcentric society. Women were property: first of their fathers, then of their husbands. They did not have the right to testify. They could not study the Torah. In this restrictive atmosphere, Jesus accepted women, honoured them, respected them and treasured their friendship. He journeyed with them, touched and healed them, loved them and allowed them to love him. There was no discrimination. For Jesus, women and men were equally capable of grasping the great religious truths, living them and announcing them to others. Mary Magdalene is living proof of Jesus' boundary-breaking humanity and compassion.

In 2016, Pope Francis announced that the liturgical memory of St. Mary Magdalene, commemorated on July 22, would be elevated to the level of a feast, like that of the other Apostles. The beautiful preface for that feast captures well Mary Magdalene's extraordinary mission to announce the Resurrection to the world. Here is my own working English translation of the Latin text published by the Vatican in 2016:

Preface of the Apostle to the Apostles

It is truly right and just,
our duty and our salvation, always and everywhere to give you thanks,
Lord, holy Father, almighty and eternal God,
whose mercy is no less than His power,
to preach the Gospel to everyone, through
Christ, our Lord.
In the garden He appeared to Mary Magdalene,
who loved him in life,
who witnessed his death on the cross,
who sought him as he lay in the tomb,
who was the first to adore him when he rose
from the dead,
and having sent her out he honoured her with her
place among the Apostles,
so that the good news of new life might reach the
ends of the earth.
And so with all the angels and saints we confess
you, in exultation singing: Holy, Holy, Holy, Lord
God of Hosts …[1]

---

1 Præfatio: De apostolorum apostola

Præfatio: de apostolorum apostola
Vere dignum et iustum est, æquum et salutáre,
nos te, Pater omnípotens,
cuius non minor est misericórdia quam potéstas,
in ómnibus prædicáre per Christum Dóminum nostrum.
Qui in hortu maniféstus appáruit Maríæ Magdalénæ, quippe quae eum diléxerat
vivéntem,
in cruce víderat moriéntem, quæsíerat in sepúlcro iacéntem,

"Doubting Thomas" or "Honest Thomas"

A proverb says, "When the heart is not applied, hands can't do anything." It seems as if this were written for Thomas the Apostle! John's first appearance of the Risen Lord to the disciples is intense and focused, a scene set with realistic detail: it is evening, the first day of the week, and the doors are bolted shut. Anxious disciples are hermetically sealed inside the room. A suspicious, violent world is forced tightly outside. Jesus is missing. Suddenly, the Risen One defies locked doors, locked hearts and locked vision. He simply appears. Gently, ever so gently, Jesus reaches out to the broken and wounded Apostle.

"Doubting Thomas" is often used to describe someone who refuses to believe something without direct, personal evidence: a skeptic. It refers, of course, to Thomas, one of the Twelve, whose name occurs in all the Gospel lists of the Apostles. Thomas is called *Didymus*, the Greek form of an Aramaic name meaning "twin." When Jesus announced his intention of returning to Judea to visit Lazarus, Thomas said to his fellow disciples: "Let us also go, that we may die with him" (John 11:16). It was Thomas who, during the great discourse after the Last Supper, raised an objection:

ac prima adoráverat a mórtuis resurgéntem,
et eam apostolátus offício coram apóstolis honorávit ut bonum novæ vitæ núntium
ad mundi fines perveníret.
Unde et nos, Dómine, cum Angelis et Sanctis univérsis tibi confitémur, in exsultatióne
dicéntes:
Sanctus, Sanctus, Sanctus Dóminus Deus Sábaoth.

"Lord, we do not know where you are going. How can we know the way?" (John 14:5).

Little else is recorded of Thomas the Apostle in the New Testament; nevertheless, thanks to John's Gospel account of Jesus' meeting with Thomas (John 20:19-31), we have a better understanding of his personality than that of some of the other Apostles. Thomas would have listened to Jesus' words, and he certainly experienced dismay at Jesus' death.

That Easter evening when the Lord appeared to the disciples, Thomas was not present. When he was told that Jesus was alive and had shown himself, Thomas said, "Unless I see the mark of the nails in his hands, and put my finger in the mark of the nails and my hand in his side, I will not believe" (John 20:25). Eight days later, Thomas made his act of faith. He hesitatingly put his finger into the wounds of Jesus and love flowed out. He is blessed beyond belief for his sincerity. Jesus exclaims to him, "Have you believed because you have seen me? Blessed are those who have not seen and yet have come to believe" (John 20:29).

Thomas, the Honest Lover

Thomas the Apostle is one of the greatest and most honest lovers of Jesus, not the eternal skeptic or the bullish, stubborn personality that Christian tradition has often painted. This young Apostle stood before the cross, not comprehending the horrors of what had happened. All his dreams and hopes were hanging on that cross. Thomas rediscovered his faith amidst the believing community of

Apostles and disciples. This point must never be forgotten, especially in an age when so many claim that faith and spirituality are attainable without the experience of the ecclesial community. We do not believe as isolated individuals, but rather, through our baptism, we become members of this great family of the Church.

Centuries after Thomas, we remain forever grateful for the honesty and humanity of his struggle. Though we know little about him, his family background and his destiny, we do know that his name means "twin." Who was Thomas' other half, his twin? Maybe we can see his twin by looking in the mirror. Thomas' other half is anyone who has struggled with the pain of unbelief, doubt and despair, and has allowed the presence of the Risen Jesus to make a difference.

Long ago, St. Gregory the Great said, "If, by touching the wounds on the body of his master, Thomas is able to help us overcome the wounds of disbelief, then the doubting of Thomas will have been more use to us than the faith of all the other apostles."

Peter's Rehabilitation and Ours

One of my favourite New Testament stories took place on the northwest shore of the Sea of Galilee, also known as the Sea of Tiberias (John 6:1) and the Lake of Gennesaret (Luke 5:1). Commemorated at the Franciscan church of The Primacy of Peter, it recalls John's post-Resurrection narrative (John 21:1-19), set against the backdrop of the Sea of Galilee.

This "sea" is really a freshwater lake in the shape of a small harp that is 12 to 13 miles long and 7 to 8 miles wide. Fish and fishing played an important role in the New Testament and in the early Church. Fishing eventually became an important symbol of the Church's missionary task, since Jesus had invited his earliest disciples to "fish for people" (Matthew 4:19; Mark 1:17; Luke 5:10). There is clearly something "fishy" about the origins of Christianity!

An Easter Brunch by the Sea

Chapter 21 is an epilogue to the Fourth Gospel, a play with two scenes. The first scene (John 21:1-14) describes the appearance of the Risen Jesus to his disciples "by the Sea of Tiberias." It is concerned with fish and fishing. When Peter decides to go fishing, there is a certain feeling of resignation and bleakness about it, alluding to the depression and discouragement he and the other disciples must have experienced after Jesus' death. Peter is simply taking up his old profession.

Jesus' appearance is shrouded in mystery, in the familiar atmosphere of "not knowing who he was" that we see so often from the Gospel writers. The disciples have been out at sea that night "but caught nothing" (21:3), a graphic portrayal of barrenness and futility. They have done what they thought was the right thing, but experienced failure. This prepares them to learn one of the central lessons of discipleship: apart from Jesus, they can do nothing (15:5). The turning point comes early in the morning, perhaps symbolizing the dawning of a new light. Jesus is described again as simply standing there, without any description of his arrival at that spot (21:4; 20:14, 19, 26).

Jesus takes the initiative and calls out to the disciples, "Children, you have no fish, have you?" (21:5). The disciples admit they have failed at fishing, and Jesus calls to them, "Cast the net to the right side of the boat, and you will find some" (21:6). They could easily have understood this remark as the idle suggestion of a bystander. But he does not say, "Try over there and you might find some!" He doesn't offer a suggestion; he gives a promise that they will find fish where he directs them to cast.

When the disciples come ashore, they notice a charcoal fire, with bread and fish prepared (21:9). There is no indication of where Jesus got the bread and fish; the appearance of the food is as mysterious as his own. The only other charcoal fire mentioned in the Gospels is the provocative scene from Luke's Passion narrative when Peter disowns Jesus (Luke 22:55). That scene presents the fire of denial and betrayal. John's Gospel story on the seashore offers the fire of repentance and recommitment.

The meal referred to may have had Eucharistic significance for early Christians, since John 21:13 recalls John 6:11, which uses the vocabulary of Jesus' action at the Last Supper. The next scene is one of great awe, with none of the disciples daring to ask Jesus, "Who are you?" (21:12). There was something different about him, yet they were able to recognize him. Now it is the Lord Jesus who is the focus of the story. After breakfast, Jesus speaks to Peter. Throughout this story, Peter has been referred to as Simon Peter, or simply as Peter (21:7a), the name Jesus had given him (1:42; cf. Mark 3:16; Luke 6:14). Now Jesus calls him by his former name – Simon, son of John (21:15) – as if he were no longer (or not yet!) a disciple.

Peter's rehabilitation and new role

The second scene (21:15-23) presents a poignant dialogue between Jesus and Peter. This is one of the most personal and moving vocation or commissioning stories in the Bible, concerned with sheep and shepherding. Peter certainly knew failure along the road of discipleship. The disciple who was called "rock" wept with regret in Luke 22:62 after denying his Lord. Now Peter is given an opportunity to repent and recommit himself to Jesus.

Three times, Jesus questions Peter and then gives a command. His question is the ultimate question in life: "Do you love me more than these?" (21:15) Does "these" refer to the net, the boats, the material things of fishing? No. By "these," Jesus probably means "these other disciples." According to the other Gospels, Peter had boasted that though all the others might fall away from Jesus, Peter would not (Matthew 26:33; Mark 14:29; Luke 22:33). John evokes this aspect, even though Peter's actions in swimming to shore and hauling up the net by himself reveal his bold character.

Within this translation of Jesus' question of whether Peter truly loves him are two verbs for love: "truly love" (*agapao*) and "love" (*phileo*). There is a pattern, with Jesus asking Peter twice whether he loves him (*agapao*); each time, Peter responds that, yes, he does love Jesus (*phileo*). The third time, Jesus switches to using Peter's word. Peter's three-fold denial of Jesus during the trial and crucifixion is now cancelled out by this three-fold declaration of love.

In response to the searing, painful third question, Peter says, "Lord, you know everything; you know that I love you" (21:17). After each profession of love, Jesus gives a command: these are similar, but use different words. First, Peter is to feed lambs (21:15); then he is to shepherd sheep (21:16). The third command includes a word from both of the previous commands, feed and shepherd (21:17), tying the three commands together.

Peter's qualifications for ministry

Why does Jesus ask Peter, on whom he is going to confer the pastoral office as chief shepherd, these questions and not others? What about asking him about his suitability for ministry? For example, "Simon, son of John, are you aware of the great responsibilities you are undertaking?" "Do you know your weaknesses?" "Can you explain your track record?" "Are you aware of how many people around you need help?" "Can you respond to all the demands that will be made of you?"

In our day, where proficiency and efficiency seem to be at the top of the list of "professional" ministerial aptitudes, we might translate those questions into the language of age and agility, academic qualifications, psychological balance, previous leadership experience, financial management, success in public relations, eloquence, diplomacy, and so on. Such questions may be important for effective ministry today. But Jesus sums them all up in a single basic question, repeated with two different verbs in Greek to indicate the nuances of love and friendship he is referring to: "Simon, son of John, do you love me? Are you really my friend?" This question goes directly to a person's heart.

The key qualification for the Petrine ministry, and for all ministry in the name of Jesus Christ, is a love for the Lord that is characterized by humility, dependence and obedience. Peter already had a devotion to Jesus, but was still full of self-will and thrusting himself to the front. Such a proud attitude of heart would spell disaster for the community, as was evident throughout Israel's history – right up to those who had just crucified Jesus. In fact, it is evident in the history of the Church to this day!

Peter learned his lesson, as is clear from the words of his first letter in the New Testament. When he addresses the elders of the communities, he does so as a fellow elder. He encourages them to "tend the flock of God that is in your charge, exercising the oversight ... Do not lord it over those in your charge, but be examples to the flock. And when the chief shepherd appears, you will win the crown of glory that never fades away" (1 Peter 5:2-4). This is authority that is exercised in humility and conscious of the Chief Shepherd. Such are marks of an authentic leader.

Ultimate responsibility for the flock

Once Peter's love has matured, he allows the Risen Lord to look into his heart: "Lord, you know everything; you know that I love you" (John 21:17). Only when Peter allowed Jesus to forgive him would he receive his new responsibility for the flock. For Peter, insight into Jesus' true identity and his compassion brought new demands and responsibilities. Peter is truly a model for us, as he must always remember his own failures as he undertakes leadership within the Church. Rather than incapacitating him, his remembrance enables him to be a merciful and compassionate leader.

Questions for reflection

- How do I deal with memories of my own failures as I reach out to others?

- Into what kind of intimacy is God calling me at this moment in my life? With whom is God calling me to be intimate?

- What do I understand to be my responsibilities following upon my own declaration of faith in Jesus?

- Peter learned his lesson well; he would imitate Jesus the rest of his life. Am I prepared to do the same?

- What competes with my love for Jesus? Do I love Jesus more than "these"?

5

Jerusalem,
City of the Resurrection

For Christians, Jerusalem is the city of the death and Resurrection of Jesus, the centre of history and of the world. It is also the city whose name evokes the new city of the future: the New Jerusalem, as mentioned in the book of Revelation, chapter 21. John's wild dream speaks of a city from God, by God and with God. The author describes the New Jerusalem as the goal of human history. Jerusalem is to be a model for what life with God will be "in the end."

St. Cyril, bishop of Jerusalem (349–384 AD), had the unique privilege of presiding over the church in Jerusalem immediately after the completion of the buildings begun during Constantine's reign. Cyril is the envy of every bishop, pastor, chaplain, parish council, finance committee and pastoral minister. Imagine walking into a situation where everything is newly built and no fundraising drives or building campaigns are needed! He preached magnificent sermons within feet of the actual places of Christ's death and Resurrection. Cyril said of Calvary, "Others only hear, but we both see and touch." He wrote, "Here in this city of

Jerusalem the Spirit was poured out on the Church; here Christ was crucified; here you have before you many witnesses, the place itself of the Resurrection and towards the east on the Mount of Olives the place of the Ascension."

In the Diary of Egeria (or Etheria), written by a wealthy Spanish woman while making her pilgrimage to the Holy Land between 381 and 384 (a trip that also included Sinai, Egypt, the Valley of Jordan, and the Transjordanian region), we read not only about her vivid impressions of the biblical sites, but also her observation of the liturgy celebrated in the shrines. She describes in detail the Sunday and weekday celebrations throughout the liturgical year, focusing especially on the Holy Week prayers in which she participated in Jerusalem. From Egeria's Itinerary we learn how she enjoyed the cordial reception of local Christians who met all her needs as a pilgrim, showing her biblical sites, conducting appropriate acts of worship in those places, escorting her, offering hospitality and advice. Her positive experiences might resemble those shared by most pilgrims at the end of the fourth century, and by pilgrims today who have the privilege of meeting the local peoples of the Holy Land.

Another pious practice linked to the pilgrimages was settling in the Holy Land. Some pilgrims set out for the land of Jesus to live there, or during their sojourn made up their minds to remain there. Such was the case of St. Jerome and his women companions. After arriving in Palestine in 386, he established a community in Bethlehem. Jerome would exclaim in his writings, "Here, he was wrapped in swaddling clothes; here he was seen by shepherds, here he was pointed out by the star; here he was adored by the magi." Jerome later wrote to his friend Paula in Rome, urging her to come and live in the Holy Land. He wrote, "The whole mystery of our faith is native to this country and this city." Nowhere else in our Christian experience can make this claim. No matter how many centuries have passed, and no matter how far Christianity has spread, Christians are wedded to the land that gave birth to Christ and Christianity.

In our day, Jerusalem and the Holy Land are torn apart by violence, intolerance and injustice. Those struggles are real, and as Christians we pray for peace and understanding to touch the land of Jesus. But this place is not to be defined by the current conflict. By seeing Jerusalem as the city of the future, we can see beyond the human failures that have led to the divisions there.

Living in Jerusalem

The final part of my graduate studies – over four years – was spent in the very city of the death and Resurrection of Jesus. In the midst of the Church of the Holy Sepulchre in Jerusalem is the tomb of Jesus, a shrine to the Risen Christ. He is not there. He is among us! I visited that holy place hundreds of times. I can assure you that all around that tomb are the remnants of over two thousand years of human discord, chaos and corruption. No matter how many structural uplifts and restorations have been carried out in the Lord's sepulchre, it still leaves much to be desired.

Nevertheless, it is the most important shrine and holy place for Christians because of the events that transpired there.

The Resurrection of Jesus is the sign that God is ultimately going to win. At Calvary, and elsewhere throughout the Church, corruption and discord seem rampant. However, on the night when the Lord broke the bonds of death, we know deep within that God is ultimately victorious. I know this within my flesh and bones, in my heart of hearts, because 70 feet away from Calvary there is a tomb that is now empty. God shall win, and shall conquer sin and death. As Christians, we have an even deeper message – not only is God going to win, but we in Christ will also win. Holy Week and Easter will never be the same for me because of those years in the Holy Land. The Easter mysteries give us a new identity and a new name: we are saved, redeemed, renewed; we are Christian, and we have no more need for fear or despair. The tomb could not hold the Lord of Life.

If the Resurrection were meant to be a historically verifiable occurrence, God wouldn't have performed it in the dark without eyewitnesses. Resurrection was an event transacted between God the Father and God the Son by the power of God the Holy Spirit. Not a single Gospel tells us how it happened. We don't know what Jesus looked like when he was no longer dead, whether he burst out of the tomb in glory or emerged like Lazarus, blinking his eyes with wonder against the dawn of Easter morning. But we must never forget the Holy City where those decisive, earth-shattering events took place. It is the City of God, God's sanctuary, the place where every believer – Jew, Christian or Muslim – has heard the Word of God, and because of that, wishes to adore God. For Christians, Jerusalem was and remains the Mother Church, the birthplace of the first Christian community. We are forever connected to that mysterious and awesome place.

A wonderful rabbinic saying from the Babylonian Talmud (Kiddushin 49b) reveals heaven, earth and Jerusalem as the essential components of the Hebrew soul. The rabbis say:

> As the world was being created, God gave out 10 portions of joy to the world and nine were given to Jerusalem; 10 portions of beauty God gave to the world and nine were for Jerusalem; 10 portions of suffering God gave to the world and nine were for Jerusalem.

Jerusalem is the city where the joys, aspirations and pains of humanity converge. It is the city where dreams are dreamt and either realized or shattered. A well-known medieval map shows Jerusalem and Solomon's Temple at the centre of the world, with the continents of Europe, Africa and Asia fanning out from there like gigantic petals. It is a vision of world redemption arising from Jerusalem. Jerusalem is the heart of the world and the centre of history. The Nobel Prize laureate Elie Wiesel touched upon this theme with his description of the holy city:

> JERUSALEM should be everywhere and
> JERUSALEM IS everywhere where a person strives

for PEACE, where the heart is opened to PRAYER, to GENEROSITY, to THANKSGIVING.

The Church is the community of those who have the competence to recognize Jesus as the Risen Lord. It specializes in discerning the Risen One. As long as we remain in dialogue with Jesus, and connected with the Mother Church in Jerusalem, our darkness will give way to dawn, and we will become "competent" for witness. In an age that places so much weight on competency, we would do well to focus every now and then on our proficiency, competence and ability to discern Resurrection.

Questions for reflection

- [If I have visited Jerusalem] How did being in the Holy City and visiting key sites in the life, death and Resurrection of Jesus affect my faith?

- Even if I haven't been there, how does Jerusalem show me personally what life will be with God "in the end"? Do I feel any connection to Jerusalem? Do I feel any desire to visit there?

- How can a connection with the earthly Jerusalem help me in my faith journey?

- How do I picture the New Jerusalem? What does it look like to me?

- Do I truly believe that God and God's way will win out over evil? How do I live out that belief?

A Prayer at the End of the Journey

Stay with us, Lord, for it is evening and
the day is far spent.
Just as the two disciples prayed on that evening
in Emmaus,
Help us to be focused and centred on you,
Our Lord, our hope, and our life.

When doubt and despair fill our lives, stay with us, Lord.
When sadness and emptiness tempt us to believe
that you are absent,
Fill us with your consoling presence.

When selfishness prevents us from reaching out
to others,
Teach us your art of selflessness.

Stay with us, Lord,
And help us to remember that the royal road of the Cross
Is the only way for us and for the Church.

Stay with us, Lord, along the journey,
And help us to discover you each day
In the breaking and sharing of the Word and the Bread.

Stay with us, Lord, as we journey to the New Jerusalem
Where you are light, peace, and endless home.
Amen.

Epilogue

Contemporary Witnesses
of the Resurrection

In the New Testament, the basis of faith in Jesus Christ is found in the eyewitness testimonies of the Resurrection. Jesus reminds his apostles that they are to be his witnesses (Luke 24:48; John 15:27; Acts 1:8). The meeting with the Risen Lord in John's Resurrection account is the humble yet powerful beginning of a new age: fear is transformed into joy; pain is changed to peace and trust; hiding and flight become courage and mission. Division and hatred are vanquished by the gift of the Holy Spirit – by God's love revealed in Jesus and through his power to remove evil and sinfulness. Jesus breathing on them (John 20:22) recalls Genesis 2:7, where God breathed on the first man and gave him life. Just as Adam's life came from God, so now the disciples' new spiritual life comes from Jesus. This action is also reminiscent of the revivification of the dry bones in Ezekiel 37. It is the evangelist John's version of Pentecost.

"Peace be with you" is the greeting and gift of the Risen Lord. The Hebrew word *shalom* means re-establishing the full meaning of things. Biblical peace is not only a pact that allows for a peaceful life, or indicates the opposite of a time of war. Rather, peace refers to the well-being of daily existence, to one's state of living in harmony with nature, with oneself and with God. Concretely, this peace means blessing, rest, honour, richness, health and life. The gift of peace that Jesus entrusted to his first disciples becomes a promise and a prayer shared with the entire Christian community.

The Holy Spirit renewed the Apostles from within, filling them with a power that would give them courage to go out and boldly proclaim that "Christ has died and is risen!" Frightened fishermen have become courageous heralds of the Gospel. Even their enemies could not understand how "uneducated and ordinary men" (Acts 4:13) could show such courage and endure difficulties, suffering and persecution with joy. Nothing could stop them. To those who tried to silence them they replied, "We cannot keep from speaking about what we have seen and heard" (Acts 4:20). This is how the Church was born, and from the day of Pentecost she has not ceased to spread the Good News "to the ends of the earth" (Acts 1:8).

But the male Apostles were not the only ones who saw the Risen Lord. Mary Magdalene and Mary the mother of James were the first to see him in his new form. Paul lists several witnesses (1 Corinthians 15:3-8). Among Jesus' disciples, there were 500 other witnesses. The accounts of these witnesses have lived on for over two thousand years. They have stood the test of time. Many who were the first witnesses to the Resurrection endured martyrdom because they refused to deny Jesus' Resurrection. They were ready to give witness to Christ in the face of intense persecution, even if it cost them their lives. The stories of their heroic lives and deaths inspired the first Christians, and continue to motivate and inspire us today. From the stoning of Stephen to the hundreds of contemporary Christian martyrs, these stories from around the world and through the ages lead us to greater faithfulness to the way of Jesus, reminding us what costly discipleship looks like in any age.

Resurrection is never an isolated, private, hidden incident. Men and women of the Resurrection motivate others to do something new. Resurrection gives meaning and joy in the midst of anguish, violence, grief and suffering. If we believe in the Resurrection of Jesus, we beg to differ with the darkness and the night. We never accept unjust situations the way they are. We become pilgrims and leaders of processions of life, ready to intersect with the many processions of death around us. We risk touching the dead and the outcasts – all those who sit in the shadows of death and exist on the peripheries of life.

Two outstanding witnesses of the Risen Lord

I have dedicated this book to Joseph Bernardin and Basil Hume, two outstanding witnesses of the Risen Lord who were leaders of processions of life – priests, shepherds, bishops and Cardinals of the Roman Catholic Church in my lifetime. Through their priestly and episcopal ministries, they risked touching the dead and the outcasts and reached out to many on the peripheries of life and the margins of the Church. They loved many grieving, suffering people back to life by restoring them to communities and circles of life. I had the privilege of knowing both of them personally. Each man left a deep and lasting impression upon me as a young man preparing for consecrated life and priestly ministry. It was not only their Gospel-rooted, prophetic ministries that taught me, but especially the ways they endured physical suffering, illness, diminishment and death. Both died before the eyes of the world, teaching us as much about living as they did about dying. Both were witnesses to the Lord's Paschal mystery, which they lived in their own bodies. They knew the Risen Lord, and their friendship with him was contagious.

Cardinal Joseph Bernardin (1928–1996)
Archbishop of Chicago, USA (1982–1996)

Joseph Cardinal Bernardin's gentle leadership throughout his priestly and episcopal ministry made him an internationally beloved figure. He lived his episcopal motto each day: "As those who serve." His great humanity marked his last months no less than his earlier career. The Cardinal began a new phase of his ministry with the diagnosis of cancer in June 1995. By September of that year, after undergoing surgery and an intensive cycle of chemotherapy and radiation treatment, he returned to work, but with an additional ministry to hundreds of cancer patients and to the dying.

"I came to believe in a new way that the Lord would walk with me through this journey of illness," he wrote in a pastoral letter on health care.

"A Sign of Hope: A Pastoral Letter on Healthcare,"
by Joseph Cardinal Bernardin,
October 18, 1995 (Archdiocese of Chicago)

He told interviewers of his nighttime fears, his bouts of weeping – but also of an abiding trust in God that enabled him to see "death as a friend, as the transition from earthly life to life eternal."

In early August 1996, less than two weeks before he learned that his cancer was inoperable, he announced a plan to bring together Catholics with different points of view, to counter the polarization he feared was blocking candid discussion of problems imperilling the Church. The Cardinal's abilities as a reconciler were rooted in his personality, which blended the prudence and precision of a painstaking administrator with the calm and patience of a man of prayer. But it was the words he left behind about his final journey that would change the lives of millions more people from all faiths, from all backgrounds and from all over the world.

In the last two months of his life, the Cardinal made it his ultimate mission to share his personal reflections and insights as a legacy. *The Gift of Peace* reveals the Cardinal's spiritual growth amid a string of traumatic events: a false accusation of sexual abuse; reconciliation a year later with his accuser, who had earlier recanted the charges; a diagnosis of pancreatic cancer; surgery; the return of cancer, now in his liver; and his decision to discontinue chemotherapy and live his remaining days as fully as possible. In the pages of that brief, yet powerful, book, Bernardin told his story openly and honestly, sharing the profound peace he came to at the end of his life. He showed us all that one of the greatest gifts we can receive is the gift of peace – a gift that comes from God alone. Joseph Bernardin accepted that gift from God, and shared it with the world. I have read and reread his book many times over the past twenty years, and have shared it with countless people who are preparing for death. The Cardinal's belief in the Resurrection of Jesus is evident in this excerpt from his inspiring book:

> As I conclude this book, I am both exhausted and exhilarated. Exhausted because the fatigue caused by the cancer is overwhelming. Exhilarated because I have finished a book that has been very important to me. As I write these final words, my heart is filled with joy. I am at peace. It is the first day of November, and fall is giving way to winter.

Soon the trees will lose the vibrant colors of their leaves and snow will cover the ground. The earth will shut down, and people will race to and from their destinations bundled up for warmth. Chicago winters are harsh. It is a time of dying.

But we know that spring will soon come with all its new life and wonder. It is quite clear that I will not be alive in the spring. But I will soon experience new life in a different way. Although I do not know what to expect in the afterlife, I do know that just as God has called me to serve him to the best of my ability throughout my life on earth, he is now calling me home.

Many people have asked me to tell them about heaven and the afterlife. I sometimes smile at the request because I do not know any more than they do. Yet, when one young man asked if I looked forward to being united with God and all those who have gone before me, I made a connection to something I said earlier in this book. The first time I traveled with my mother and sister to my parents' homeland of Tonadico di Primiero, in northern Italy, I felt as if I had been there before. After years of looking through my mother's photo albums, I knew the mountains, the land, the houses, the people. As soon as we entered the valley, I said, "My God, I know this place. I am home." Somehow

I think crossing from this life into life eternal will be similar. I will be home.

What I would like to leave behind is a simple prayer that each of you may find what I have found – God's special gift to us all: the gift of peace. When we are at peace, we find the freedom to be most fully who we are, even in the worst of times. We let go of what is nonessential and embrace what is essential. We empty ourselves so that God may more fully work within us. And we become instruments in the hands of the Lord.

The Gift of Peace *(Loyola Press, 1997, pp. 152–153). Used with permission.*

Cardinal Basil Hume, OSB (1923–1999)
Archbishop of Westminster, England (1976–1999)

George Haliburton Hume was the first monk to be made Archbishop since 1850, when the Roman Catholic hierarchy was restored in England and Wales. At his installation Mass in Westminster Cathedral in 1976, Hume had announced a different episcopal style from that of his predecessor, Cardinal Heenan, a prince of the church. In words borrowed from St. Augustine of Hippo, Hume announced that he intended to be "a bishop for you" and "a Christian like you." His episcopal motto summed up poignantly his life: *Spes inter Spinas*, "Hope among Thorns."

Cardinal Hume's episcopal ministry saw Catholicism become more accepted in Britain than it had been for 400 years. The nation and the world looked to this Benedictine monk for spiritual leadership. He served for 23 years as Archbishop of Westminster, which he thought too long, and in his final years was plagued by depression. At the end, Hume found that his prayer was "amazingly sweet, full of consolation." Then, in his own words, "the curtain came down." But, he said, "I wasn't worried, because I knew what was behind the curtain."

His deep, faithful prayer life gave him much resilience. His writings influenced millions of people around the world and became essential reading for young religious, like myself, who benefitted greatly from his spiritual wisdom and his understanding of the human condition. He deplored a tendency that grew worse in the following years: "The spirit of the Pharisee lurks in each one of us, myself included, tempting us to sit in judgment on others and even to seek to exclude them from the church."

During my years of graduate studies in Rome, the Cardinal came often to the Eternal City during Lent to preside at a penance service for anglophone priests at the English College. Many of us would go to confession to this good and holy man, who was always dressed in his simple Benedictine habit. I shall never forget what I felt during those moments of reconciliation with him. Basil Hume knew about the human condition, about the desire for God and about loneliness – "that most common affliction of priests," as he called it. He had embraced celibacy as enabling a special gift of the self, but he was frank about the cost. After my confession with the Cardinal, I always came away with the conviction that this man knew the Risen Jesus. A speculation about the soul before its Judge ran deep with him. In one of his meditations on the Crucified Lord, Basil Hume wrote:

> We shall approach,
> trembling
> nervous no doubt
> but reassured and at peace
> as we tell the story
> of our lives
> which only he can understand.

Basil Hume, Seven Last Words (Darton, Longman & Todd, 2009)

In 1998, Cardinal Hume asked Pope John Paul II for permission to retire, so that he could go back to his monastery at Ampleforth in England. The request was refused. He was diagnosed with inoperable stomach cancer in April 1999. On June 2 of that year, Queen Elizabeth awarded him the Order of Merit. He died in London two weeks later, on June 17, at the age of 76. Pope John Paul II said that the good English Cardinal was a "shepherd of great spiritual and moral character."

In a profoundly moving funeral homily in London's Westminster Cathedral, then-Bishop John Crowley of Middlebrough spoke of Basil's final journey:

The story of those final days is of someone almost entirely at peace, preparing himself intently for his 'new future', as he called it, in a farewell letter to his priests. When his doctors first told him of his advanced cancer, he went straight to the hospital chapel where he sat praying for half an hour. 'I had preached so often on the seven last words of Jesus from the Cross,' he said, 'now it was wonderful to find they were such a part of me.'

But then 'the curtain came down', and it was back to the darkness of faith. 'But I wasn't worried', he said, 'because I knew what was behind that curtain'. … In those final weeks, curtain up or curtain down, the Cardinal's one prayer was simply this: 'Father, into your hands I commend my spirit'.

But for the Cardinal a new future beckons. All his life he has been a pilgrim, searching restlessly for glimpses of God. 'It is your face, O Lord, that I seek, Hide not your face' (Psalm 26/27).

Now that journey is over. He is safely home behind the curtain, face to face. Our deep love for him and our deep gratitude for the gift he was provokes this final thought: If such were the gift, what must God be like, the Giver of that gift.

Cardinal Basil Hume was not afraid to meet the Risen Lord at the end of the journey. He was a witness to the Resurrection who showed us how to prepare for our final journey to the Father. He taught us not to be afraid of the One waiting for us on the other side of the curtain.

WERE NOT OUR HEARTS
GRADUALLY CATCHING FIRE
WITHIN US
AS HE SPOKE TO US
ON THE ROAD ?